Almost forgotten

YORK DAILY RECORD ■ YORK COUNTY HERITAGE TRUST

World Wide Web:
Part of this work can be accessed at the York Daily Record's Web site, www.ydr.com. For a wealth of information on York County's history and current historical celebrations, events and festivities, see the York County Heritage Trust's Web site, www.yorkheritage.org.

To contact the author:
E-mail: jem@ydr.com, or write to James McClure, York Daily Record, P.O. Box 15122, York, Pa. 17405.

To order:
Copies of this work are available through the York County Heritage Trust, 250 E. Market St., York, Pa. 17405, 717-848-1587, www.yorkheritage.org and other York County booksellers. Also, the York Daily Record, P.O. Box 15122, York, Pa. 17405, 717-771-2000, www.ydr.com. James McClure's "Never to be Forgotten," and "Nine Months in York Town" can be obtained through the same outlets. A video, "Never to be Forgotten," provides a broad view of York County history and includes segments on the county's black history. It is available at the same outlets.

Copyright ©2002. James McClure.

ISBN Number
0-9710416-3-6

Library of Congress Control Number: 2002101804

McClure, James
Almost forgotten/A glimpse at black history in York County, Pa./ [Researched and written by James McClure; Edited by Kim Strong; Design, visuals by Ted Sickler]. [York, Pa.]: York Daily Record/York Newspaper Co., [2002].

Printed on paper donated by Glatfelter, Inc.

On the cover

"The Negro's Slavery is Abolished, and the Colored population set free...," 19th-century York County artist Lewis Miller wrote beneath his drawing of a gathering celebrating the Emancipation Proclamation. President Abraham Lincoln issued the proclamation in September 1862, freeing slaves in territories at war with the Union. The proclamation went into effect Jan. 1, 1863. York County blacks did more than celebrate the freedom promised their kinsmen in the South. They marched off to war, joining what were then called colored troops to fight against the Confederate Army, contributing to the demise of the rebel forces.

On the back cover

Lewis Miller, 1796-1882, a carpenter by trade and an artist by avocation, captures a black congregation laying the cornerstone of a church on York's North Duke Street. From these early years of freedom to this day, black houses of worship in York County represent a key part of the foundation for community life.

Almost forgotten

JAMES McCLURE

"The status of African-Americans must reflect the contributions their forefathers made to the development of America. History and knowledge of the Black race will give our people a sense of direction and will bring greater respect from others, and will create a faster infusion of the Black race into the American system. I accept the term African-American, referring to the historical richness of the lands of my ancestors and the opportunities of the land of my birth."

— Wm. Lee Smallwood from introduction of "African-Americans of Note," 1991.

Contents

Credits and acknowledgments 2
Foreword 3
Introduction 4

Almost forgotten 5
 I. 1780-1860: From tillers to town toilers. 7
 II. 1861-1940: Rebs troop on York County soil 25
 III. 1941-2002: While Johnny marches, York plans
 and Rosie rivets 43
Epilogue: Never to be forgotten 67

Appendix: Behind the scenes 69
25 sites linked to York County's black heritage 70
22 Profiles in Heritage: A celebration of York County's
black history. 72
12 questions and answers about York County's
black heritage 77
9 Months in York Town: Slaves included in Continental
Congress' visit 79
1907 — The African Race in York and York County 82
1912 — The Goodridge House in York 86
1924 — Squire Braxton and Black Hester:
Two Noted Slave Characters Who Figured in
York's Early History 90
10 ways to learn more about black history
in York County 94
Other works consulted 95
Index. 96

Credits and acknowledgments

Author: James McClure
Photo/layout coordinator: Ted Sickler
Primary content editor: Kim Strong
Layout artist: Tracey Bisher Cullen
Copy editor: Deborah L. Hummel

Giving due credit

The author thanks the York Daily Record staff members listed above for their tireless work on this project.

Also, thanks to York Daily Record Editor and Publisher Dennis Hetzel for his active support of this work. And Buckner News Alliance's officers Philip F. Buckner, David B. Martens and Gail B. Brown for their interest in this and past history projects.

Thanks, too, to York Daily Record editorial assistant Loretta Martin and receptionist Donna Hollinger for helping to prepare the manuscript, photo technician Cheryl Spilman for preparing the photographs, and York Daily Record librarians Joan McInnis and Nancy Duncan for assisting in research.

Thanks to Messiah College student Joseph McClure for preparing the index and reading the manuscript.

Michael Newsome, York Daily Record controller and chair of the task force planning the 25th Annual Conference on Black History in Pennsylvania was a great encouragement on this work, as on past history projects.

Much of this work's research came from the York County Heritage Trust's Historical Society Library. Thanks to June Lloyd, Lila Fourhman-Shaull, Lamar Matthew, Nancy Amspacher and Justine Landis, all from the Heritage Trust staff, for their assistance and patience. Thanks to Gayle Petty-Johnson, president and chief operating officer, for her support of this project. The Heritage Trust has been a helpful partner on this work, as on past coordinated projects.

Wm. Lee Smallwood, a student of York County's black community, provided invaluable insight and guidance along the way. Thanks to Michelle Owens for her work on the Profiles in Heritage in the appendix.

Much appreciation to Thomas Norton, vice president of production, York Newspaper Co., for his assistance.

Purpose: The goal of this project is to enhance knowledge and understanding of York County's black history with an emphasis on everyday life. The project is presented in conjunction with the 25th Annual Conference on Black History in Pennsylvania, in York, May 2002.

Project concept: This work includes original and revised material from "Never to be Forgotten," and "Nine Months in York Town," by James McClure, plus scores of additional items and photographs prepared particularly for this work.

A point of style:
In accord with Associated Press style, the descriptive term "black" was used in this work, and "African-American," "Negro" or "colored" were used only in quotations or names of organizations.

Reviewers and readers:
The following reviewers provided countless helpful suggestions: June Lloyd and Nancy Amspacher, York County Heritage Trust. Also, Wm. Lee Smallwood, Doris Sweeney, Shirley Johnson and Voni B. Grimes.

Photo credits:
York County Heritage Trust; Murals of York Inc.; York Daily Record; The York Gazette and Daily; Wayne Ruppert Jr.; The Library Company of Philadephia; Pennsylvania State Archives; Beverly S. Osborne Pearson collection; St. Louis Art Museum, National Archives.

Foreword
Enlightening history's prism

19th-century illustration by Lewis Miller

IMAGINE holding a prism that couldn't separate all the colors to the sun. The emerging rainbow still might be attractive, interesting and even useful to those who would take the time to study it.

However, since we would never know about the missing colors, we would be misled into thinking we were seeing the whole rainbow.

That describes the way many adults learned American history in their student days. We were taught about events, dates and places connected to the things that white men did, particularly those who managed to collect enough power or wealth, or both, to make an obvious impact. Or, when women or people of color flew into the historian's radar, their roles were described to the extent they influenced the acts of white men.

Journalism, it is often said, represents the first rough draft of history. In the rush to cover the news, the easiest and most obvious approach is to report the actions and reactions of the most visible players. These actors take the main roles on the stage and, sometimes, keep others from playing anything beyond supporting roles.

Thus, it isn't surprising that, when historians blow the dust off of old news clippings, they mainly find chronicles of events through that same, useful-but-flawed prism.

I want to believe that such oversights haven't been malicious, at least much of the time. Having a point of view based on life experiences is a fate none can escape — of any color or gender. Newspapers are hardly immune.

It's a hard lesson for any organization to learn. You cannot possibly reflect an increasingly diverse community if everyone is the same — no matter how well intended you might be.

And learning from history demands as complete of a story as possible.

Those lessons were taught to York County people in difficult, tragic ways in 2001 — a year no sane person would want to relive, but a year that any sane person should want to learn from.

On the national stage, the terrorist attacks of Sept. 11 provided stark evidence of the failure to heed history's warning signals. And now we must scramble as a nation to better understand the motivations, fears, strengths and vulnerabilities of millions of those in the Muslim world who were far less important to many of us than the latest episodes of our favorite television shows.

Even closer to home, the events surrounding the investigation into York's 1969 race riots took twists and turns that have rarely been pleasant for anyone. At times, the event felt like a hurricane blowing through town with greater strength than anyone would ever have forecasted.

The good news about hurricanes is that they end. They provide opportunities to rebuild damaged structures so they'll be stronger when the next storm winds blow.

So, let's learn and rebuild. A piece of that rebuilding process is a wonderful event in 2002, the 25th Annual Conference on Black History in Pennsylvania in York.

Another piece is this book, "Almost Forgotten." James McClure, the York Daily Record's managing editor, has worked with many good people at the newspaper and throughout the community to capture the black experience in York County in a fresh, accessible way. Once again, Jim has combined his significant skills as both journalist and historian to give the community a gift of lasting importance.

So, enjoy this book. And learn from this book.

There might be colors in the rainbow that you've never seen.

Dennis Hetzel
Editor and Publisher
York Daily Record

Introduction
First friends, then history

A SOLID friendship is hard to come by today. It takes trust and respect and that intangible something that creates a strong bond.

What you hold in your hands today was born of my friendship with Jim McClure.

His deep involvement in York County history led me down a similar path and straight into the arms of a welcoming group of people, the York County Heritage Trust Board.

When that group asked me to chair a focus group charged with bringing the 25th Annual Conference on Black History in Pennsylvania to York, I accepted out of the spirit of my friendship with Jim. Frankly, history was a subject I had passionately avoided until I met Jim. With him, I was beginning to develop an appreciation for this subject and a growing desire to know more about York County's past.

Later, I asked something of Jim in return: Would he use his considerable knowledge of York County history to compile a book of black history? Some of this he had already published in his two local books, "Never to be Forgotten" and "Nine Months in York Town."

I wanted this conference to reflect the excellence for which the Trust is known. More importantly, I wanted attendees to leave York with knowledge of the rich diversity of our community — a strongly positive impression.

The bond of our friendship held strong.

Jim agreed to do the work, resulting in this rich history of black culture in York County — a segment of this community's people who have been nearly forgotten in many local history books. These pages include something about all races.

Here, you will find those forced to come to this county, those who gained prominence for their life's work, and those who live their lives by loving and working and changing. You will see a piece of yourself in its pages.

This book is not all you might want it to be. It's not all we thought it could be. It will make you mad and proud, and it will make you think about yourself and personal feelings about black people and white people. We hope it will mostly make you reflective. We hope it will open your mind to the possibilities of York County.

"Almost Forgotten" is what it says it is — a "glimpse." It's like looking through the small end of a funnel. The light is brightest at the other end of the spectrum — what you can't see, unless you come close and look with your heart. Then you will see the possibilities.

This is our invitation to you to come close — join us on this journey. Read and learn about those who looked and saw the possibilities in York County. Those that were, but for two friends, almost forgotten.

Michael Newsome
Controller
York Daily Record

Almost forgotten

These studio shots from old scrapbooks at the York County Heritage Trust's Historical Society Museum show two faces of York County. Left: From the Harriet Johnson collection. Right: Part of the Heritage Trust's 'A Place to Call Home' exhibit.

Suppose you find a dusty photo album on an attic shelf. As you open it and turn the pages, the snapshots tell a story.

The first photos show family members when they were young. As you move through the album, you see them age. One generation fades with the birth of the next.

The photo-filled pages appear as chapters, providing a snapshot of all kinds of events. The family at work. At play. Celebrating. Grieving.

This album covers but a few milestones in the family's life. There is not space for everything. But those snapshots pasted before us speak much about the family.

What you are holding here is a photo album, showing snapshots from York County's past. The photos speak about the hearty people and families who lived before we did on the west bank of the Susquehanna River and points westward.

We can learn much from their rich past. Their lives. Their accomplishments. Their deaths.

Never to be forgotten passages that are almost forgotten.

Chapter I: 1780-1860
From tillers to town toilers

York merchant William C. Goodridge regularly introduces new products for sale and advertises them in newspapers. This illustration comes from such an ad. The figure demonstrating a hair product is believed to be Goodridge.

This is a story about how skyscrapers grow from York County's cornfields.

First come the sea-weary farmers and tradesmen eager to work after months crossing from Europe. Often, they settle on eastern Pennsylvania farms before a growing population pushes them to the shore of the Susquehanna. Others come directly from seaports to the Susquehanna via foot or wagon. They ferry across it, stake out their acreage and begin tilling the rich limestone soil of York County's rolling countryside. Sometimes they buy slaves or secure indentured servants to increase their household productivity.

Indeed, about 4,000 slaves were transported to Pennsylvania by 1730, and 471 bondsmen were living in York County in 1783.

Then, some sons of these tillers step away from the country homestead and work at trades as a primary means to support their families. As the 1700s slip into the 1800s, those trades turn products of the land into marketable goods: iron-making, carpentry and tanning. These tradesmen depend less and less on slave labor.

Slavery is gradually abolished in Pennsylvania after 1780, and an increasing number of freedmen call York County home. Not all 19th-century tradesmen have tap- roots in the county's deep soil.

William C. Goodridge, born a son of a Maryland slave and trained as a barber, settles in York and rises with the county's developing merchant class. The presence of barbers in York County suggests that some county residents now have disposable coins to pay a tradesman to shear their hair and provide a shave.

Goodridge soon offers other wares. He raises a building of five stories, a skyscraper in those days. The Goodridge emporium houses his barbershop, newspaper distributorship and other retail shops. The former slave also owns railroad cars and reportedly uses them to transport runaway slaves as part of the Underground Railroad.

Goodridge's house, on York's East Philadelphia Street, and other county houses are also thought to be part of the underground network that helps freedom-seeking slaves make their way as far north as Canada. With the blood of slaves in his veins, Goodridge is vulnerable to capture if the Confederate Army moves north of the Mason-Dixon Line. But his business continues on as the rebels come knocking on York County's western door in June 1863.

The entrepreneur says goodbye to York County, probably sometime in 1865.

1780: Philadelphia
Blacks gain liberty a little at a time

Philadelphia merchant William Frampton secures six slaves from the African coast in 1685.

Thomas Taylor, master of the ship Isabella, writes to Frampton that the slaves are available for him to "dispose of & sell them to the best advantage… ." Cargoes or parcels of slaves, as they are called, become part of Pennsylvania's commercial activities until at least 1766.

Slavery is an integral part of Pennsylvania's economy, providing hands and backs to alleviate a shortage of colonists to do necessary work. Historian Leroy Hopkins observed that the number of slaves held later becomes a status symbol. "As such, it is not surprising," Hopkins said, "that slavery would be taken to the frontier by pioneers who could benefit from its dual function." In those days, York County is such a frontier.

But by 1773, abolitionist Anthony Benezet writes that the number of slaves imported into the province had declined so much that "more are sent off than are brought in."

In 1780, Pennsylvania adopts a gradual emancipation law, which provides that people bound to slavery before 1780 would remain so, but those born after March 1, 1780, would become free upon reaching the age of 28. The deadline for owners to register their slaves is Nov. 1, 1780. Those not entered on the slave register by that date would be considered free.

"No other single law or action in this period would have a greater impact on the lives of Afro-Americans," Debra Newman Ham, a York native and professor of history at Morgan State University, stated. "One of the cogent reasons for the passage of this law was the effort of the Pennsylvania abolitionists to erase the contradiction that the institution of slavery caused in the American people's struggle for independence from England."

The census of 1790 shows that 3,737 persons are held in bondage in the state. Reports concerning the number of slaves in the town of York range from 28 to 43 in 1780.

Just a few years before, that number had swelled when the Continental

George Washington is believed to have visited York County at least four times. His last visit came in 1794 when America's first president worked to quell the Whiskey Rebellion in western Pennsylvania. Lewis Miller, 3-years-old when Washington died in 1799, probably never saw the president but the York artist draws him here as a young American offers him a drink. In his will, George Washington, a slaveholder as an 11-year-old after his father's death in 1743, arranged for the slaves he owned to be freed. His wishes were carried out, and the 123 bondsmen at his Virginia home, Mount Vernon, gained their freedom.

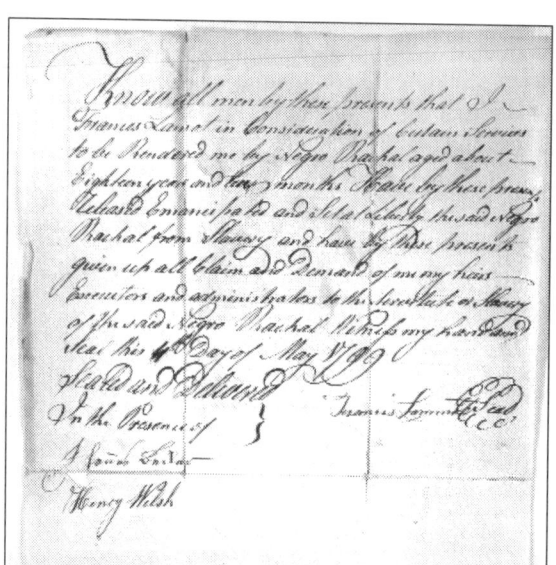

Francis Lammot of York County signed this document releasing and freeing his slave Rachal, May 4, 1799. Pennsylvania's gradual emancipation law helped reduce the number of slaves in York County from 499 in 1790 to 77 in 1800. York County was one of the largest slaveholding counties in Pennsylvania.

Congress met in York for nine months in 1777-78. Slaves and servants accompanied some of the delegates and members of the military.

1783: Hellam Township
Some freed, others unlucky

Most slaves are held outside the town of York.

A county tax list details that Hellam Township, the county's oldest municipality, founded in 1739, contains 16,037 acres of inhabited land, 101 dwellings, 86 barns, eight mills, 345 male and 320 female adults, and seven slaves.

In York County, which includes present-day Adams County, 471 slaves are counted in a census in 1783. In 1790, York County ranks second to Philadelphia statewide in size of black population and also size of free black population. In that year, census figures report 499 slaves; in 1800, 77; 1810, 22; 1820, six.

York County's last slave, an unknown bondsman owned by a Forney family of Hanover, is thought to have died in 1841.

1792: Danville, Vt.
The stands of Stevens

Thaddeus Stevens, a fervent abolitionist and controversial figure in 19th-century America, is born in New England.

After graduating from Dartmouth, his first stop is the York County Academy, where he teaches for a year starting in 1815 while studying law. He apparently forms enemies in York, and he reportedly is rejected in a bid to join the Freemasons. Further, county lawyers pass a resolution forbidding anyone from taking the bar exam who is not studying law full time.

Stevens also works around a residency requirement of two years by passing his bar requirements in Bel Air, Md. He leaves York to practice law in Gettysburg, where he becomes a leading Pennsylvania lawyer.

Stevens' accomplishments include his defense of public education as a member of the state Legislature and his abolitionist voice as a member of the U.S. Congress.

"To some he was the 'Old Commoner' or 'Great Leveler,' who fought for the poor, the oppressed, and the underprivileged," a historian said, "by others he was held in great contempt as a clubfooted, evil, vengeful politician who climbed to power by shrewdly supporting the issues that were popular with the lower class of voters of his day."

1795: York County
Of slaves and servants

Notices for runaways in The Pennsylvania Herald and York General Advertiser suggest that some slaves and black indentured servants in Pennsylvania and Maryland in the late 18th century have a variety of linguistic skills.

In one notice, Phil Gartner of York says Tom Cotton, a runaway, can speak English and German and plays the violin.

Another runaway must have been articulate on religious matters because an advertisement notes he tries to impersonate a minister. Another runaway, Jonathan Jackson, is described as a fiddler. Kitty, "Negro Wench," speaks English, German and "a little French." She is presumed to have a pass for a "free Wench," and "it is supposed she has been with child since the Run Away, she is able to deceive any person."

During their indentures, most servants could not marry, vote or otherwise participate in the political process.

In 1800, the five Jacobs brothers were well-known in York County. Top, Lewis Miller drew, from left, Laurence, a blacksmith; Stoffel, a cabinetmaker; John and Jonathan, both farmers; and Michael, a carpenter. The York natives were the children of a German, 'Old Jacobs,' and his wife, a mulatto. Miller noted that the brothers were old men by 1800. Two never married, and three had wives and children. Right, in another drawing, Miller captures three of the brothers in different attire.

1803: York County
'Conspiracy of 1803'

Arsonists set fire to several barns and residences in York after a black woman is convicted for trying to poison two white York residents. The plot is discovered after about three weeks, and several blacks and whites are arrested. Six blacks receive prison sentences. Here, in the Lewis Miller drawing, York's town fathers arrest the conspirators, forcefully bringing them into the criminal justice system.

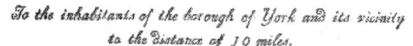

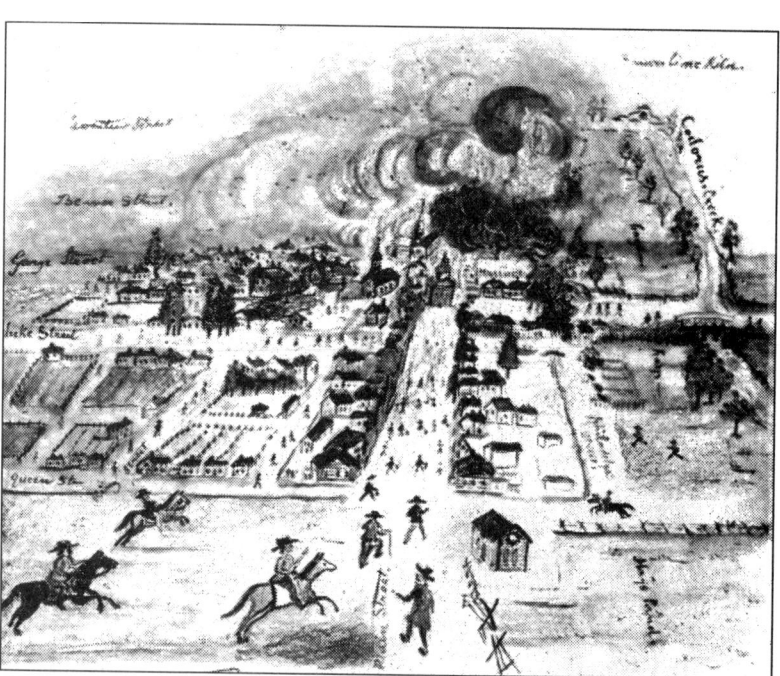

York authorities issue this flier, called a broadside, in English and German, putting forth restrictions on slaveholders, their bondsmen and daily travel of freedmen.

A large fire burns in York, evidence of the 'Conspiracy of 1803.' Six black men and women were found guilty for their role in the arson plot and sentenced to serve prison sentences. Eleven blacks and one white man were found not guilty.

1803: York County
Mysterious York barn fires end in multiple arrests

Barns and some houses mysteriously burn in the York area until the "Conspiracy of 1803" plot is discovered.

Arsonists torch the buildings following the conviction of Margaret Bradley, a black woman, for allegedly trying to poison York residents Sophia and Matilda Bentz.

The plot is discovered when a girl tries to ignite a fire at a barn owned by a Mr. Zinn at noon rather than at midnight.

"So secret and artful was the conspiracy, that though the fires were known to be the work of incendiaries, yet no suspicion was for a long time attached to the blacks of the place," a historian wrote. "On nearly every successive day, or night, for about three weeks, they set fire to some part of town... ."

Whites are involved in the arsons, too. "(A) number of suspected blacks and whites have been apprehended and committed to jail," a petition from York residents to Gov. Thomas McKean stated, "and some since their commitment, have made confessions, which being the offense named to them: it is strongly suspected that many of our worthless white people, are involved in the combination."

Eleven blacks are found not guilty as was at least one white man, John Foulks. Six blacks are found guilty and sentenced to the Walnut Street Prison in Philadelphia: Isaac, slave of Peter Dinkle; Isaac, servant of Margaret Spangler; Abner; Hetty Dorson; Ruth and William Grimes. Some defendants are sentenced to hard labor and solitary confinement for extended periods.

The court scolds the local abolition society for providing asylum "for many vile, worthless black people, fugitives from a neighboring state."

During the height of the conspiracy, borough authori-

George Spangler apprehends 'his black boy Abe' at Peter Reisinger's blacksmith shop. Abe was suspected to be part of the plot to burn barns and other buildings in the York area. Arson was considered a serious crime, often a crime of revenge, and the criminal justice system took such charges seriously.

ties issue a notice to residents of York and its vicinity within a 10-mile radius: "You are hereby notified, that such of you as have Negroes or people of colour, to keep them at home under strict discipline and watch; so as they may be under your eye at all times. You are not to let them come into the borough of York on any pretense whatever without a written pass... ." That notice addresses slaveholders. As for free blacks, they are notified to get a pass from the justice of the peace "in order that they might not be restrained from their daily labor."

1804-05: York County
Bertholff's strange send-off

Baron de Beelen Bertholff and his wife fall victim to a contagious disease, perhaps yellow fever.

The Bertholffs had come to York County in the late 1700s from the Low Countries in Europe to promote commerce with America. Bertholff's work had benefited the foreign trade of both America and Europe.

A man transports Bertholff's body in a coffin from York to Conewago Chapel in Adams County, but leaves the coffin standing in front of the church. Fearing the disease, people allow the royal body to stay there all day.

Two black men helped resolve the quandary.

"Toward evening Father de Barth (the local priest) sent over to the Lilly farm for help," a history stated, "and two colored men came and assisted him in the last sad duty in the burial of the once distinguished man."

1806: York
Goodridge's works help him succeed

William C. Goodridge is born in Maryland, and his mother's slave master-physician apprentices him as a boy to a York pastor-tradesman.

Goodridge works in the Rev. Michael Dunn's tanning yard until 1822, when he receives his freedom, a suit of clothes and a Bible. Goodridge follows a career path open to blacks, training as a barber in Marietta, Lancaster County.

He returns to York to establish a hair-cutting business by 1824. Goodridge marries Evalina Wallace, a Maryland native, and the couple develops wide-ranging business ventures in York.

"During the quarter century following their marriage (in 1827), William and Evalina Goodridge established themselves in York as members of southeastern Pennsylvania's emerging African American elite," a historian said. "They were an effective team."

A newspaper advertisement in 1827 touts Goodridge's barbershop. The barber's business is a constant for Goodridge. One of his last ads in

Goodridge

1800s: York County
Everyday life

Lewis Miller's father was schoolmaster at York's Christ Lutheran Church school, so Miller was familiar with Sunday happenings at the church. He shows a black man kneeling on the stairway, left center, in this 1800 scene. Some York blacks went to the churches of their masters, and others met in homes before black congregations more formally came together to worship after 1811.

Lewis Miller drew this elderly black woman spinning at a wheel. The woman's name was 'widow herman or Eduie,' Miller wrote. The woman had been in jail on murder charges. 'She was sentence to be hung and Governor Snyder give her mercy,' Miller wrote.

1865 promotes Goodridge's shaving and hair-cutting business. Its services include the sharpening of razors, scissors and surgical equipment and the procurement of human hair. The hair perhaps is used to make or repair wigs.

Other Goodridge ads promote a line of stoves, fresh fruit, "cheap jewelry," perfumes, hair dye, cosmetic paints, guitars, accordions and "harmonical fifes." An advertisement in 1832 pushes a bathhouse at the rear of his shop: "It is in a perfectly private situation, and persons wishing to bathe can be supplied, at a moment's warning, with perfectly pure water, either cold or hot, as they may desire... ."

Goodridge enterprises also include an employment office (called an intelligence agency), a pay-to-view Christmas tree in his home and a rail line. Goodridge rail cars run from York to Philadelphia.

Goodridge lays out his entire business line in his advertising, except, of course, his role as a stationmaster on the Underground Railroad.

His role in helping fugitives to freedom extends to the radical abolitionist movement. Goodridge reportedly hides Osborn Perry Anderson, a conspirator in John Brown's raid on Harpers Ferry, W.Va., in 1859, on the third floor of his Centre Square building. After several weeks, Anderson moves to Philadelphia in a Goodridge rail car and then to freedom in Canada.

When Evalina Goodridge died in 1852, a newspaper remembered her as assisting "her husband materially in his business at York."

1809: York
Showing the way to freedom

William C. Goodridge is not alone among blacks in aiding runaways to gain freedom along the Underground Railroad.

Susan Marrs, born in York in 1809, is another. "Susie" Marrs works for the prominent York families of James Lewis and Charles Barnitz. While at Barnitz's Springdale home, Marrs assists in producing silk, setting up mulberry trees to bed the silkworms. (The worms feed on mulberry leaves.)

She and her brother-in-law, John

A black youth, an apprentice to blacksmith Jesse Hines, lends a hand in fixing a pale fence. Miller notes that no two pales are alike in the 200-foot-long fence on South Duke Street. Here, Hines is frustrated because the rail is rotten. When he nails in one clapboard, a half dozen fly off.

Johnson, hide runaway slaves until it is safe to guide them to the Susquehanna River and freedom in Canada. "Miss Marrs was one of the most respected and trusted women of her times," a newspaper reported.

A father and son also reportedly work to free slaves. John Mars starts the work and his son, James, follows his father. James later moves to New York City and continues his abolitionist work there. He gains prominence as a bank executive and earns the friendship of Abraham Lincoln.

Another prominent black citizen, William Wood, helps conduct the Underground Railroad "secreting the escaped slaves to prevent them from falling in the hands of their brutal masters… ," a newspaper reported.

Wood, a machinist, is employed in the York machine shops of inventor Phineas Davis. He is credited with working on some of Davis' innovations, including the first successful coal-burning steam railroad engine in the United States.

1811: York
Congregation meets in homes

Seventeen black citizens of York gather in their homes for religious worship, forming a congregation.

Their first church building, secured in 1811, is a one-room structure on North Duke Street. The church later starts a day school for black children.

More than 50 years later, a building committee composed of Aquilla Howard, Greenberry Robinson, Isaac Golden, Richard Wilson and James Smallwood arranged for the construction of a building on East King Street, between Duke and Queen streets. This church also was used as a school for black children, and James Smallwood served as principal and teacher for more than 25 years.

Later, the Smallwood School, an all-black school that became part of the York City School District, was established in the 200 block of South Pershing Avenue. The Aquilla Howard School, also a school for black children, was constructed on the 400 block of East King Street.

Today, Small Memorial African Methodist Episcopal Zion Church, located on South Queen Street, traces its lineage to this 1811 congregation. The church is named for the Rev. John B. Small, a former pastor and bishop.

At least two black African Methodist Episcopal Church congregations met in York early in the 19th century.

The A.M.E. Zion church was founded in New York City in 1796. "Zion" was added to its name in 1848. Today, Small Memorial A.M.E. Zion Church is a member of this denomination.

Another A.M.E. denomination grew out of the Rev. Richard Allen's work in Philadelphia. The Rev. Allen was the first black person ordained by famed Methodist missionary and bishop

'Fanny Dock again,' artist Lewis Miller writes. 'A fight on the Common on a muster day old Fanny Dock & Superon, a German teacher, 1810.'

Francis Asbury. A conference in Philadelphia elected the Rev. Allen as the first bishop of the newly organized A.M.E. church in 1816.

Today, York's Bethel A.M.E., West Princess Street, is part of this denomination.

c. 1814: Prince Georges County, Md.
Slave destined for history

Caroline Craig is born into a slave family on a small plantation.

She stays on her master's plantation as both Union and Confederate troops camp on its grounds during the Civil War.

Fifty-five years after the war ends, the 106-year-old ex-slave cast a ballot in the General Election of 1920, the first time women could vote.

One historian claimed that Caroline Craig, then a resident of Oak Lane in York, was the oldest woman in the United States to cast a ballot.

1817: York
Sunday schools teach reading

Twenty-six children attend the county's first Sunday school.

The early schools teach young people to read and become acquainted with the Bible. Instructors caution against Sunday tavern-haunting, riding horses, swimming in the Codorus Creek, or engaging in profane or political conversation.

The educated and moneyed at first treat the movement with disdain but later support it completely. One of the early schools meets at the York County Academy, indicating that the educated are starting to see the movement's benefits to better young people.

Sunday schools provide the only educational opportunities available to some children.

By 1819, 19 schools operate in the county, including one black school. Blacks initially find themselves excluded from the Sunday school movement, contrary to the organization's constitution.

The Society of Friends reacts by opening a summer Sunday school for black people in the home of Paraway Lewis. The Rev. Samuel Bacon, promoter of the local Sunday school movement, also teaches a night class for black people.

Today, hundreds of Sunday schools meet each week in the county.

1819: York
Reports of female trouble

Lydia Profet, listed as "colored," is charged with using the Bible to tell fortunes but is found not guilty of the blasphemy charge.

"The jury acquitted the defendant," the newspaper reported, "and she was discharged with an admonition from the court, warning her to cease from evil ways, as she would certainly not always escape with impunity, if she persisted in them."

Other women run afoul of the law in these days. Elizabeth Mullen, a white woman, is convicted in 1820 of keeping a "disorderly house," perhaps a euphemism for a brothel. A judge sentences her to pay a $10 fine and spend four weeks in jail.

Domestic discord is evident, too. Five times from 1815-1820, spouses publish notices in The York Gazette that they are disclaiming responsibility for their wives' debts.

1819: York
Abolitionists call for members

Amos Gilbert, Charles Morris and William H. Brown are among leaders of the York County Abolitionist Society.

They declare themselves available to provide information to others who are against slavery.

"It has been suggested that a number of persons friendly to equal rights," a notice in a York newspaper states, "would wish to become members of the Abolition Society if they knew when and where to apply."

The only expense connected to membership, the notice said, is a $1 annual dues.

1820: Liberia, Africa
York Co. man dies in Africa

The Rev. Samuel Bacon, former York County Academy teacher, attorney and recently ordained Episcopal priest, dies of fever in Liberia.

Bacon was working with the

American Colonization Society. This group persuaded Congress to purchase land along the African coast, called Liberia, to populate with freed blacks.

Some York County residents are not willing to assimilate freed slaves into the community. They fear black people would fill scarce jobs.

For example, when 52 ex-slaves from Virginia arrive in York in 1819, a newspaper reported, "These may be … but the harbingers of numerous other bodies of these unfortunate people. All is consternation and conjecture here."

The newspaper speculated that some in Virginia are sending their freed slaves north out of resentment toward local abolitionist societies interested in making York County another Sierra Leone, an African colony founded by a philanthropic company as a home for freed slaves.

A week later, the newspaper observed that the slaves, directed by their "conductor," John Crew, passed through York to Columbia in Lancaster County, where that town's abolitionists are caring for them.

Bacon

The ex-slaves are well clothed, decent and worthy candidates for colonization in Africa, the newspaper said. After dispersing the manumitted people across Pennsylvania, it would be difficult to collect them again particularly because freed slaves in the state are not favorable to colonization.

"The Virginians," the newspaper added, "had better keep their black flocks together, until the colonists are ready to ship them off, in case they do not, the colonization business will have an insurmountable obstacle thrown in its way by the refusal of the blacks to go to Sherbro (an African colony)."

The Randolphs, Greens, Pleasants and Haydens are among the descendants of these 1819 Virginians. Another group of 100 freed slaves comes in 1821. Some stay in York, and others settle in Columbia and Marietta.

1800s: York County
Everyday life

Lewis Miller draws Eleanor Smith, wife of York County's Declaration of Independence signer James Smith, accompanying a child. 'Mrs. Smith taken her colour'd boy Able to Miller's School,' Miller wrote, 'learning him to read and write.' Johann Ludwig Miller, the artist's father and schoolmaster at the Lutheran Parochial School, taught the boy in the evening by himself — not to interrupt the day school.

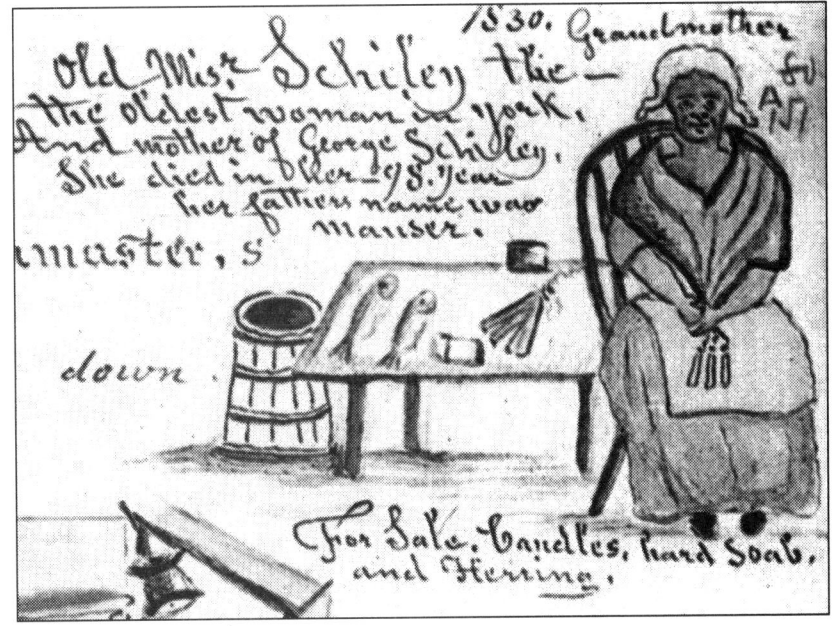

Miller captured what appears to be a black woman near a table bearing candles, soap and fish. Miller wrote: 'Old Mrs. Schiley, the oldest woman in York and mother of George Schiley. She died in her 98 year, her father's name was Mauser.' Miller noted that she operated a small store.

1820: York County
Ads run to find runaway slaves

Between 1815-1820, out-of-state slave owners place about 15 ads seeking the return of their runaways in The York Gazette.

One ad promises a $40 reward from a Frederick County, Md., slave owner for a "Negro Man" named Bill.

County residents also seek the return of indentured servants. Shoemaker Thomas Miller offers 6 cents and an old shoe for runaway Joseph Collins. Clement Stillinger offers a 1-cent reward for return of an apprentice carpenter "no thanks given for bringing back the said runaway."

Whether real or exaggerated, many stories surround the quest to capture runaway slaves.

For example, two Southerners find three of their escaped slaves working for a Quaker near York. "Will thee come into the house and have some dinner before thee goes?" the farmer asks. The farmer and two daughters entertain the slave catchers while a third daughter helps the slaves escape.

In 1826, two Marylanders seize a freed black man near Columbia and attempt to sneak their victim through the county. At Abbottstown in Adams County, some local residents prove him legally free. The incident prompts indignation after the man is made to walk 25 miles back home in the January snow.

A runaway slave is shot near Lewisberry, and the slave catchers return the severely wounded man home as a warning to other slaves. The slave dies of his wound. Albert Ridgely, a slave catcher, shoots and kills William Smith of Columbia in 1842, claiming he is an escaped slave from Harford County, Md. Ridgely successfully flees to Maryland, despite pursuit from York County's sheriff. Ridgely overextends himself and dies in Baltimore.

Another captured slave believes his master will sell him to a new owner in Georgia. Determining to end his usefulness, the jailed man somehow fetches an ax and deliberately chops off his left hand at the wrist.

William Yocum, a constable, is known to join in slave hunts and deliberately steer slave catchers away from their prey. One time, Yocum helps hide a party of 16 slaves. When it is safe, the party crosses the Susquehanna River on horses one November evening.

When the last fugitive crosses, one of those who helped the party proclaims, "Great God! Is this a Christian land, and are Christians thus forced to flee for their liberty?"

Old 'Jonne Erven,' a native of Guinea, kneels and prays. He lived at the corner of Market and Beaver streets in York.

Above, four men try to help out an elderly black woman who slipped down a well. Lewis Miller wrote, '1813 — Fanny Dock fell in the well in S. Water Street. John Brown, John Kaufman, Adam Kaufman, Jacob Siechrist secured her from drowning....' This incident must have fascinated Miller. He produced a second drawing of the same subjects. In that drawing, Dock is shown walking away from the well, alive and well. Left, The York Gazette often published notices placed by owners of runaway slaves. This advertisement appeared in 1816.

ALMOST FORGOTTEN

1829: York
G.J. Goodridge first of photographers

Glenalvin J. Goodridge, later York's first native son to establish a lasting photo studio, is born to William C. and Evalina Goodridge.

Glenalvin Goodridge teaches at the school for black children in York and takes up part-time work as a daguerreotypist in 1847, one of only five or six blacks known to have worked as photographers before 1850.

Goodridge reaches his pinnacle when he wins first place in a photography competition at the York Fair in 1856.

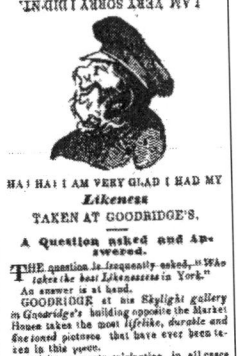

This clever advertisement told two different messages, depending on which way the reader held the newspaper.

His low point comes in 1862, when he is convicted of rape and sentenced to five years in Eastern Penitentiary in Philadelphia. More than 100 of York's leading citizens petition the governor for Goodridge's release.

The petition includes the arguments that the alleged victim waited three months after the attack to report it, Goodridge produced a credible alibi, the jury took 20 hours to reach a verdict, and the conviction would not have occurred if the defendant were white.

The support moves Gov. Andrew G. Curtin to action. He pardons Goodridge after two years in prison.

But in confinement, Goodridge had contracted tuberculosis. The disease claimed his life in 1867.

GOODRIDGE'S AMERICAN PHOTOGRAPHIC GALLERY,

GOODRIDGE'S BUILDINGS, CENTER SQUARE, YORK, PA.

The Subscriber offers to the public a New Style of

LIKENESSES,

Being far superior to the Daguerreotype or Talbotype; they are termed

AMBROTYPES.

The process for which is patented in the United States, England and France, and the subscriber holding the exclusive right for York county, therefore they cannot be obtained at any other Gallery in York county but his. These pictures are the most beautiful and truthful ever produced by the Photograpic Art and WILL LAST FOR AGES UNCHANGED. The public are cautioned against spurious imitations made on glass that are not as perfect as ordinary Daguerreotypes.

G. J. GOODRIDGE.

RECOMMENDATIONS.

"GOODRIDGE'S AMBROTYPES—We have seen several very excellent pictures taken by G. J. Goodridge, by the new process termed Ambrotyping. These pictures are taken upon plates of glass prepared in a manner similar to the plates prepared for Daguerreotyping, and upon this a plate of glass of the same size is hermetically sealed, rendering the pictures indestructible by ordinary usage or by the effects of age.

"The Ambrotypes resemble well finished steel engravings—the glare of the Daguerreotype is entirely obviated, and they strike the eye in the most agreeable manner.

"GOODRIDGE'S establishment is in Goodridge's building, Center Square, where these pictures may be seen and examined, and where Likenesses will be taken at all times, either by the old or by the new method, on the most reasonable terms."—*People's Advocate*.

Glenalvin J. Goodridge, eldest son of York entrepreneur William C. Goodridge, regularly advertised his photographic services in newspapers and other publications. Here, he places a notice in the York City directory in 1856.

1825: Newberry Township
Brothers guilty in slave's assault

Four slave-hunting brothers severely wound a runaway in a chase on Joseph Garretson's land. Garretson employs George, the runaway, at the time the Fetrow brothers come calling.

The hunters present a printed advertisement offering a $100 reward as authorization for nabbing George. The case ends up in court, where presiding Judge Walter Franklin holds that the ad does not provide the Fetrows with authority.

A jury declares three of the brothers guilty of riot and assault and battery.

1827: York County
Black Hester gains renown

Two wagons carrying about 50 freed blacks rumble into York from Leesburg and Alexandria, Va. The freedmen climb out at Penn Common.

The Rev. John Joyce, a local black pastor, initially cares for the newcomers and asks leading residents of York for help. The women often gain jobs as untrained nurses, cooks and household attendants; the men find places as servants.

Charles Granger, one of the passengers, works as a servant for about 10 years and then returns to Penn Common. He builds a hovel there, and accompanied by a dozen dogs, collects garbage and other waste material for compost. He sells it to townspeople for their gardens.

When Squire Braxton, as Granger was called, died in 1881 at the age of 97, 500 people came to the graveside service. "Thus ended the career of a colored man known for half a century by all the people of York," a newspaper reported.

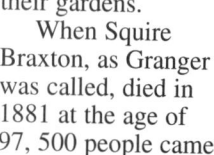
Black Hester

Black Hester gains local renown for her good voice, quality household work and reputation for baking the best gingersnaps and Maryland biscuits around. "Why bless you," she would say, noting that it isn't hard to beat bakers in York. "They know how to bake bread, but Hester can beat them making sponge cake, big ginger cakes and the tiniest sugar cakes you ever saw."

When the 94-year-old became ill in 1880, more than a dozen women visited her home to make her comfortable. The Rev. John B. Small, noted minister, preached at her crowded funeral.

Other freed Virginians who became known around the community: Zach Shaw, Charlie Shaw, Black Simon, Dosey, Black Rachael and Sally Ruddens.

1834: Columbia
Property of blacks target of damage

Several incidents in which whites damage the property of blacks break out in 1834 and 1835 in Columbia, a town across the Susquehanna River from Wrightsville that is commercially connected to York County.

Stephen Smith, a former slave who had become wealthy in the coal and lumber businesses, is the target of several attacks.

Smith receives a letter suggesting that he make his presence scarce in Columbia: "You must know that your presence is not agreeable, and the less you appear in the assembly of the whites the better it will be for your black hide, as there are a great many in this place that would think your absence from it a benefit, as you are considered an injury to the real value of property in Columbia."

William Wright, John L. Wright and James Wright, prominent businessmen and Smith's friends, place a notice in the Columbia Spy stating that the threat had injured them, too, and offered an award for the author of the letter. There are no reports that Smith received any more harassment.

But in 1842, Smith, now ordained as a minister in the African Methodist Episcopal Church, moves to Philadelphia, tired of the persecutions lodged against him.

1837: York County
Court hears slave case

A county court case involving a runaway slave ends in the U.S. Supreme Court.

Margaret Morgan, the runaway, lives with her children in York. Edward Prigg, an agent for her slave master, seizes her without securing his rights from the proper authorities.

This violates the state law against kidnapping. Prigg is convicted and appeals his case to the Supreme Court.

In 1842, the Supreme Court rules that states are exempt from enforcing the Fugitive Slave Law of 1793, which provided for the return of slaves who escaped to free states.

Since Pennsylvania and York County law enforcement officials are no longer required to aid in catching slaves, more fugitives head north, and the Underground Railroad comes under sharper attack in the South.

The federally imposed Compromise of 1850 offsets the Prigg case by introducing the Fugitive Slave Law. This legislation forbids Northerners from harboring slaves and creates a federal enforcement system to catch escaped slaves.

1837: Maryland
Smith born in slavery

Amanda Berry Smith, a future nationally prominent missionary, evangelist and singer, is born a slave in Maryland.

The historical marker, located today at the former Grace United Methodist Church in Shrewsbury, cites her accomplishments:

Smith

"Her father bought the family's freedom, and they moved to a farm near here. While still a child she was converted at this church. She committed her life to missionary work and traveled in the U.S. and to Britain, India, and Africa. Published a monthly paper, 'The Helper.' Founder and superintendent, Industrial Home for Colored Children in Illinois."

1800s: York County
'Fillis' and Mrs. Kelly

Lewis Miller shows Fillis, a black woman seen here smoking a pipe, holding a bird while Mary Kelly applies paint to it. Miller notes that Mrs. Kelly painted the bird for fun. One local history states that Fillis may have been the slave of Thomas Kelley, who lived near Laurel, and later lived with the family of James Kelly, Thomas Kelly's son, in York. James Kelly was Mary Kelly's husband.

Fillis carries some turpentine to sprinkle on bugs eating cucumber plants as Mary Kelly and Robert Wilson converse about the problem.

1845: York
New mode of transit opened

A wagon apparently bearing boxes of furniture pulls into York from the direction of Baltimore.

The man at the reins falls in a fit, and someone curiously raises the lid of one of the boxes. He sees a woman packed inside.

"She, of course, went her way… ," a newspaper reported.

The Baltimore Sun filled in some details about the woman. The slave girl had belonged to Benjamin Ross and had been missing for some time.

"It appears from the facts which have transpired that she was safely delivered in York, Pa., as per invoice," the newspaper said, "snugly packed away in a good sized box adapted to her dimensions."

1846: York
Black Masons march in York

Blacks from across the region march with 31 of their brethren from the Codorus Lodge, the local black Masonic chapter.

Glenalvin J. Goodridge, a teacher in the local school for black children, presents a banner to Codorus Lodge for its charity work, particularly toward widows and orphans in the community.

The procession and prior meeting at the Philadelphia Street lodge are without incident in a day when some townspeople could show antipathy toward both blacks and members of Masonic orders. Some Christian denominations opposed freemasonry and other secret societies.

"We are pleased to state that the best order prevailed throughout — no insult was offered — and in the evening, although the town was full of colored strangers, there was not the least disturbance," a newspaper reported.

1847, 1850: York
Buildings rise high

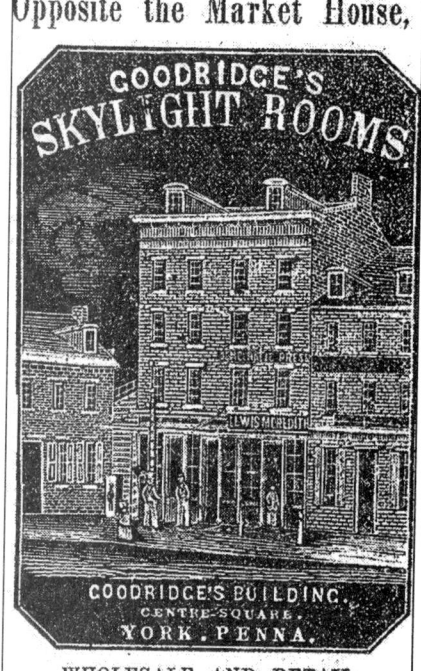
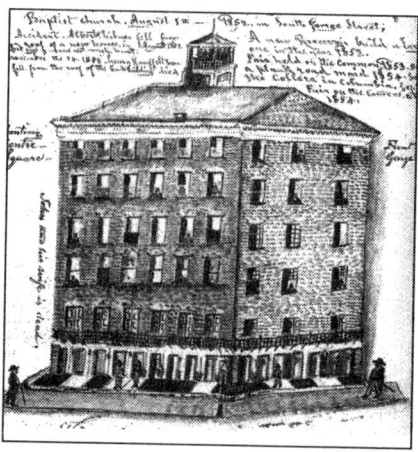

These two buildings in York scraped the sky better than any others. Left, William C. Goodridge's five-story emporium was built on the northwest corner of Centre Square in 1847. Above, John Hartman built a six-story building on the southeast corner in 1850. Today, the Hartman Building, chopped in height since then, houses Futer Bros. Jewelers. The Goodridge building has long been demolished.

1849: York
Mott gives Sabbath address

Lucretia Mott, one of the foremost abolitionists of her day, speaks at the Society of Friends meeting house on a Sunday and the York County Courthouse the next day.

"All the leading people of the town and surrounding country who opposed slavery came to hear her eloquent words," a historian later wrote.

William Lloyd Garrison, famed abolitionist and anti-slavery journalist, spoke in 1843 to audiences in Lewisberry and York.

1851: York
G.J. Goodridge marries Rhoda Grey

Glenalvin J. Goodridge marries 16-year-old Rhoda Cornelia Grey, daughter of Hamilton and Jane Grey.

The Greys were from Maryland and came to York in the mid-1840s. Hamilton Grey, a laborer, owned real estate valued at $1,800, which might have been "Mr. Erb's Stage Stable" in York.

"…Glenalvin's and Rhoda's marriage was more than a personal union in that it further cemented the bonds between two of York's well-established African American families," a historian wrote.

Prominent families of both black and white races in York are strongly connected.

"Rhoda was a first cousin of Ralph Toyer Grey of Baltimore, who would marry Glen's sister Emily O. Goodridge in 1855. And, in fact, when Emily traveled west to join her husband in Minneapolis, it was in the company of Hamilton W. Grey, Rhoda's brother, who had returned east that year to marry Mary Smallwood, a Goodridge neighbor in York," the historian noted.

1851: York
First Baptist church meets

First Regular Baptist Church starts meeting on the third floor of the Hartman Building on York's Centre Square.

It is the first Baptist congregation in York. The church is integrated — two of the 13 charter members are black.

Blacks worshipped at First Baptist until 1883, when they formed Shiloh Baptist.

Religious activities were integrated at times in the county.

When slavery was legal, some black people attended church with their masters. In 1772, the rector at St. John's Episcopal Church baptized five white and two black adults.

In 1879, the Sunday School superintendent at Stewartstown Presbyterian Church wrote about a church social: "People, little people, big people, young people, old people, black people, white people, snarling snappish people, and rollicking, rumping, merry, glossy-headed, dancing eye people, all felt the inspiration of the occasion… ."

1851: Lancaster County
Riot tests slave law

The Christiana Riot in Lancaster County provides a landmark test of the federal Fugitive Slave Law.

The 1850 law forbids Northerners to harbor slaves and created a federal system to nab the runaways.

The riot occurs a year after the law is passed. Edward Gorsuch, a Baltimore County farmer, learns that four of his runaway slaves reside in Christiana. Gorsuch and his son, Dickinson, accompanied by a U.S. marshal, travel to Christiana and demand the return of his slaves.

He comes face to face with William Parker, a leader among area black people. A melee breaks out, Edward Gorsuch is killed. His body is returned to his home via the Northern Central Railroad in York.

Dickinson Gorsuch is beaten so badly that he spends months recuperating in a York home.

Thirty-eight defendants are arrested, but none are convicted for the act. Parker escapes after the riot.

Parker could tell an interesting tale about his flight to freedom from the South through York County to

c. 1853: York
School board appoints new teacher

Frances Ellen Watkins Harper, later the leading black American poet and anti-slavery advocate, is found qualified to teach in the school for black children in York.

School directors found Harper qualified to instruct in geography, grammar, arithmetic, reading, writing and orthography.

She receives $20 per month for assuming the position formerly held by Glenalvin J. Goodridge.

In York, she reflects on whether she should continue teaching or move into the anti-slavery field. She later chooses the abolitionist path.

Harper

She observes the Underground Railroad in operation in York, which had a lasting impact on her long career as a poet and activist:

"I saw a passenger per the Underground Railroad yesterday; did he arrive safely? Notwithstanding that abomination of the nineteenth century — the Fugitive Slave Law — men still determine to be free. Notwithstanding all the darkness in which they keep the slaves, it seems that somehow light is dawning upon their minds."

'The Slave Mother'

Heard you that shriek? It rose
So wildly on the air,
It seemed as if a burden'd heart
Was breaking in despair.

Saw you those hands so sadly clasped —
The bowed and feeble head —
The shuddering of that fragile form —
That look of grief and dread?

Saw you the sad, imploring eye?
Its every glance was pain,
As if a storm of agony
Were sweeping through the brain.

She is a mother, pale with fear,
Her boy clings to her side,
And in her kirtle vainly tries
His trembling form to hide.

He is not hers, although she bore
For him a mother's pains;
He is not hers, although her blood
Is coursing through his veins!

He is not hers, for cruel hands
May rudely tear apart
The only wreath of household love
That binds her breaking heart.

His love has been a joyous light
That o'er her pathway smiled,
A foundation gushing ever new,
Amid life's desert wild.

His lightest word has been a tone
Of music round her heart,
Their lives a streamlet blent in one —
Oh, Father! must they part?

They tear him from her circling arms,
Her last and fond embrace.
Oh! never more may her sad eyes
Gaze on his mournful face.

No marvel, then, these bitter shrieks
Disturb the listening air:
She is a mother, and her heart
Is breaking in despair.

— *Frances Ellen Watkins Harper, undated.*

Lancaster County.

As the story goes, a large county resident attempted to capture him. The white man reached into his pocket as if to draw a pistol and grabbed at Parker with his other hand. Parker struck him with a heavy stick, apparently breaking his arm. When nearing Columbia, Parker and his runaway brother heard men coming behind him. They hid to let them pass, and Parker recognized his master's voice. For such deeds, Parker gains a reputation for boldness among whites and blacks.

The Christiana Riot serves as a lightning rod in the slavery debate. Abolitionist forces argue the riot shows the weakness of the law. Pro-slavery forces contend the North is shrugging at the law.

Federal marshals help slave owners recover 332 fugitives during the 1850s.

1855: Wrightsville
Disturbances hit churches

Some slaves traveling on the Underground Railroad stay in Wrightsville and worship with long-time black residents in a new brick church on Orange Street.

Rural black churches meet in the Lower Chanceford, Fawn Grove and Delta-Peach Bottom areas.

Intruders are known to disturb the meetings of black congregations. After an incident in 1867, a Wrightsville newspaper reported: "Last Sabbath the act was repeated and interrupted the meeting to a great extent, and when the persons, so badly disposed, were approached, they beat a hasty retreat." The newspaper carried a warning that future offenders would be prosecuted.

Another interruption occurred at a Delta revival meeting in 1902. A constable approached the church with handcuffs in one hand and a revolver in the other, seeking a fugitive. Parson L.F. Whitens was exhorting unrepentant sinners to turn over a new leaf when the constable entered and stood before the escapee. The constable offered the choice of handcuffs or the contents of the revolver, and the fugitive chose the lock-up.

"The event caused so much surprise among the congregation," a historian wrote, "that the meeting was adjourned."

1800s: York County
Slavery: Myths and realities

Myth	Reality
Slavery was a Southern institution.	Slavery at one time had been legal in Pennsylvania and all other British colonies. Prior to 1780, slavery generally was accepted in York County.
York County residents were staunchly opposed to slavery.	Even though a number of York County residents were active abolitionists, most citizens were indifferent to the issues of slavery.
Most Northerners believed in racial equality.	Even though many Northerners were opposed to slavery, they still practiced racial segregation.
The Underground Railroad was a highly organized network of "conductors" and "stations."	Few areas developed sophisticated networks. Help to the fugitive slave happened almost accidentally, and sometimes consisted of no more than a little food and directions to another friendly house.
Fugitive slaves were hidden in secret compartments in "safe" houses until it was time to move on.	Fugitive slaves were hidden, when necessary, in many places — in houses, as well as barns, outbuildings, fields and secluded wooded areas.
Fugitive slaves traveled only at night under the cover of darkness.	After crossing the Mason-Dixon Line, fugitive slaves could travel at any time over open fields and public roads, meeting with little resistance. However, caution was used, as slave catchers were always a threat.
A fugitive slave's journey was over after crossing the Mason-Dixon Line into York County.	Some fugitive slaves did settle in York County to build a new life, but many continued northward and eastward to other hospitable locations, such as Philadelphia, New York, Boston and Canada.

Adapted from: York County Heritage Trust research

1800s: York County
Underground Railroad

The Willis farm

The Underground Railroad operated in York County from the late-18th century to the 1860s. The system was a loose network of people — whites and blacks of various religious denominations — and places that moved runaway slaves north to freedom, according to York County Heritage Trust researchers. By the mid-19th century, the network's operations were described in railroad terms: those giving assistance — conductors; their homes — stations; escaping slaves — cargo. 'Roads that crossed the Mason and Dixon Line north into York County as well as roads running west to east carried "cargo" through the county to scattered "stations" where the travelers could find food, clothing, medical attention and directions to another friendly house,' Heritage Trust research states. Fugitive slaves traveling from stations in Adams County often secured quarters among Quakers of Warrington Meeting. They would then cross the Susquehanna River at Middletown Ferry. The Willis farm, north of York, afforded shelter, and fugitives were reportedly hidden inside corn shocks in fields. Other known Underground Railroad sites: The Jessop and Chalfant families provided food to runaways hiding under hay in their Springwood Farm barn, along Baltimore Pike. Slaves often would cross the Susquehanna at McCall's Ferry in Lower Chanceford Township, pass through Christiana and then to Philadelphia. Others crossed at Wrightsville in railroad cars owned by William C. Goodridge, the noted black businessman in York, and boatmen sometimes rowed others across. Harriet Tubman reportedly visited York County two times, including to freed black Ezekiel Baptiste's Newberry Township farm.

Warrington Meeting House

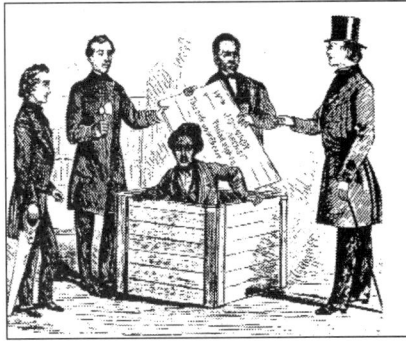

Slaves escaped the South through any number of means — draymen's carts, family carriages and funeral processions. Above, the drawing shows an ingenious ways of escape. Henry 'Box' Brown was nailed into a small box and shipped from Richmond, Va., to Philadelphia. A woman similarly escaped from Baltimore to York County in 1845. The York County Heritage Trust's Historical Society Museum has a replica of Brown's box.

The Goodridge family would hide fugitives in their Philadelphia Street home and their Centre Square store. The runaways would then be transported to Columbia in Goodridge rail cars, advertised above.

1856: Wrightsville
Former slave relishes freedom

When former slave Aquilla Howard passes the Pennsylvania line and gains his freedom in the county, he jumps off the canal boat filled with lime, grabs a handful of soil and repeatedly kisses it.

He works for P.A. Small, co-owner of York's leading business, P.A. and S. Small, for 47 years.

He carries a wreath when Abraham Lincoln's funeral train stops in York in 1865 and serves as Sunday school superintendent at Small Memorial A.M.E. Zion Church. One of York's two schools for black children was named in his honor.

When he passed away in 1923 at the age of 87, he left a lifetime of accomplishments.

Howard lived his life as if he appreciated the lime boat captain's words spoken when they crossed the Mason-Dixon Line to freedom: "Now, my man, you're in Pennsylvania and on free soil."

1856: York County
Coroner calls juries on deaths

Coroner Samuel J. Rouse calls three juries to determine the causes of death in three separate cases over a two-week period.

The first jury determines that Maria Green died from the effects of alcohol abuse. In the second case, Augustus Hartman died after falling from a railroad bridge while intoxicated.

"When found, he had in his pocket a flask filled with liquor," witnesses testify at the jury. In the last case, Stephen Brown was found dead in a stable. The jury determines that Brown died from a heart attack. Green and Brown are listed as "colored."

Coroner inquests, common in the 19th century, are rare today.

1800s: York County
Family life

Domestic work was an occupation tended to by many York County blacks in the 1800s. Here, a black woman tends to an infant in what is believed to be the well-to-do York home of Hannah Cassatt-Coleman.

1860: York County
York tops county in black residents

More than 1,200 black people live in York County, including more than 300 in the Borough of York, according to 1860 U.S. Census figures.

York County's population is 68,200.

Blacks are employed in York as shoemakers, teachers, machinists, tailors, milliners and oyster shuckers. Wrightsville shows a black census of 169.

Other large numbers of blacks live near the Mason-Dixon Line: Lower Chanceford Township, 212; Peach Bottom Township, 123; Hopewell Township, 66; and Fawn Township, 94.

Occupations in those areas include domestic help, bark grinders, boat hands and farmers.

Chapter II: 1861-1940
Rebs troop on York County soil

Artist Lewis Miller captures York's fathers meeting the Confederate Army as it marches into the borough. The rebels occupied York for two days before countermarching to join the Confederate fight in the Battle of Gettysburg.

Thousands of infantrymen in Gen. Robert E. Lee's Confederate Army march unimpeded into York in late June 1863, as the citizenry, decked in its Sunday best, heads to church. Soldiers take down the American flag from the pole in Centre Square.

Earlier, most local black people had traveled east to the safety of Lancaster County to avoid capture and the southward journey into slavery. York's fathers had headed west to Farmers along the pike to Gettysburg, met the rebels and made what they considered a binding deal: York would offer no resistance if the Confederates would not set their town on fire.

Now in town, Jubal A. Early, the commanding general, takes advantage of this deal. The town will be spared, he says, if townspeople pay $100,000 and fork over immense quantities of flour, sugar, coffee, molasses, salt, meat, food, hats, boots and socks.

York meets the food and clothing demands but raises only $28,000.

Meanwhile, Confederate Gen. John B. Gordon's brigade continues eastward in an attempt to cross the mile-long bridge at Wrightsville. Union troops offer scant resistance and skedaddle across the bridge.

The Union soldiers unsuccessfully attempt to blow up one span behind them, but the wooden structure catches fire causing a blaze seen miles away and endangering businesses and homes in Wrightsville. Confederate soldiers join local men and women in forming a bucket brigade to douse the flames.

Gen. Lee recalls the rebels from Wrightsville and York because a major battle looms west of York — in Gettysburg. Aside from the Wrightsville bridge, York County dodges major damage.

As the Confederate infantry withdraws, Union and Confederate cavalry fight saber to saber on Hanover's streets.

Union troopers keep Gen. Jeb Stuart's horsemen, the eyes and ears of the Confederate Army, from immediately joining Lee's main force. Stuart's horsemen, counting thousands in number and often sleeping in their saddles, take a wide detour. They head north through Jefferson, Dover and Dillsburg en route to Carlisle and then cut back south to Gettysburg. Lee is forced to begin battle in Gettysburg without his cavalry.

York County becomes one of the few communities north of the Mason-Dixon Line to play a role in both the Revolutionary and Civil wars. But some York residents are embarrassed that their borough — a town with strong business, cultural and family ties to the South — does not resist the rebels.

To this day, York promotes it Revolutionary War successes foremost despite a warning fro a diarist. The Confederate in sion, Cassandra Small write is "a matter never to be forgo en."

1860s: York County
Serving in the military

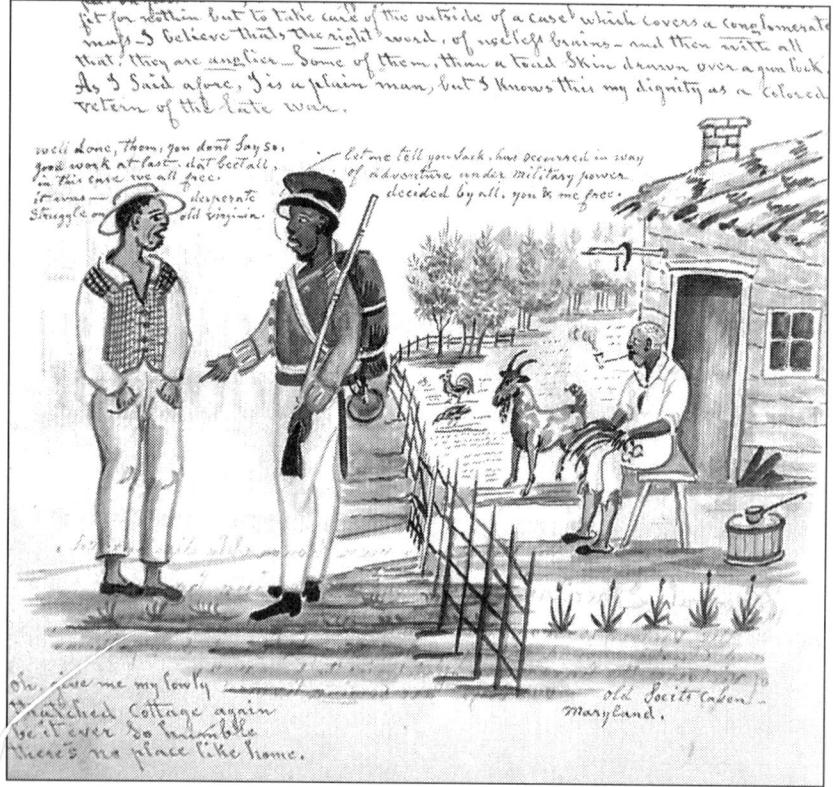

Scores of blacks from York County volunteered or were drafted to become part of the United States Colored Troops and other Union fighting units. They typically reported to Camp William Penn in Philadelphia for training and equipping. One hundred and seventy-nine thousand black soldiers and 10,000 black sailors served in the Union forces. An estimated 38,000 blacks lost their lives in uniform, either in combat or through disease. Here, artist Lewis Miller portrays a fully equipped black soldier talking with a civilian.

James Barton from Wrightsville made his mark, lower right, on this enlistment form in Carlisle. He traveled to Camp William Penn in Philadelphia for training, where he contracted a severe case of measles that impaired his health for the rest of his life. Barton recovered sufficiently to serve in the 127th Regiment, U.S.C.T.

1860, 1864: York County
County opposes Lincoln ticket

County voters favor Abraham Lincoln's opponents in U.S. presidential balloting in 1860 and 1864. The voting suggests that many county residents are voting what today would be called a centrist position. They do not support the divisiveness caused by Lincoln's anti-slavery policy.

The county has many abolitionists, and others are sympathetic to slavery, in part, because some county businesses do extensive trade with southern states.

Yet a third body of voters — perhaps a majority of the electorate — apparently believes that continuation of the Union comes ahead of resolving the divisive slavery issue. The York Gazette summarized this "Copperhead" position with the motto: "The Union As It Was, The Constitution As It Is, And the Negroes Where They Are." The centrist Copperheads look harmless (like the snake), but could actually inflict intense pain, their opponents said.

"York was distinctively Northern but not bitterly anti-Southern," York industrialist A.B. Farquhar said, years after the war. "The community felt that slavery was wrong in principle. At the same time, being acquainted with many slave owners, we also knew that slavery was better in practice than in theory and that the planter who was cruel to his Negroes was a rare exception."

Some county residents also come to personally dislike Lincoln after the incoming president fails to appear at a community party in his honor.

The president is scheduled to stop in York on his way to Washington to assume the presidency. The night before his appearance, Lincoln learns of an assassination plot in Baltimore so he passes straight through that city in the dead of night in a two-car train.

Meanwhile, York continues to prepare for his appearance the next morning. Leading Republicans wait at the station. A band plays stirring music. A four-wheeled carriage awaits the distinguished guest.

But the train pulls in without Lincoln, and the great crowd learns that the president was in Washington tending to important business.

"The disappointed crowd, headed

by the welcoming committee, quietly and slowly left the depot," an observer told a newspaper. "Thus ended the great demonstration in honor of Mr. Lincoln in York."

1863: Wrightsville
Black soldiers serve nation

When Confederate troops invade York County in the days before the Battle of Gettysburg, a company of black minutemen joins three white companies in reinforcing troops guarding Wrightsville and the bridge over the Susquehanna River.

The soldiers are provided tools to dig trenches west of Wrightsville. The white companies return to their homes while the black company digs the trenches with picks and shovels.

Upon seeing the fortifications, the approaching Confederates lob some cannon rounds into the town, killing two. A shell decapitates a black soldier in the freshly dug trenches, and a Philadelphian later dies from his wounds.

York County produces many black Civil War soldiers. Many such soldiers from Wrightsville come from the Bear, Brown, Jamison and Barton families. The Bartons produce at least seven soldiers.

Some free blacks serve as substitutes for white soldiers. A drafted resident could buy his way out of the military by cutting a deal with a substitute.

1865: York County
End of war, Lincoln killed

PROCLAMATION!

In consequence of the death of President LINCOLN, who was brutally assassinated last night, the citizens of the Borough of York, are hereby enjoined to observe the following order as a token of respect to his memory, and as an expression of their deep regret at this great and sudden calamity which has befallen the country at this critical juncture of its affairs, viz:

All places of business to be closed at 12 o'clock, for the remainder of the day.

The Bells to be tolled from 1 to 2 o'cl'k this afternoon.

Flags to be put at half-mast, and draped in mourning.

DAVID SMALL,
Chief Burgess.

York, April 15, 1865.

Chief Burgess David Small sets forth in this broadside how the Borough of York would remember President Abraham Lincoln, felled by an assassin's bullet the day before.

1864: East Saginaw, Mich.
Goodridge brothers open photographic studio

Living in East Saginaw, Mich., Wallace L. and William O. Goodridge, sons of William C. Goodridge, officially reopen the photo studio that had been closed in York.

These pioneering black photographers are later joined by their brother, Glenalvin, upon his release from prison after a pardon on a rape conviction.

The studio remains in the family until Wallace's death in 1922, earning the Goodridge family the reputation for running what has been described as the most significant and enduring black photography business in the United States.

By 1867, William C. Goodridge, the former York businessman, is residing in Minneapolis, with his eldest son, Glenalvin, who dies that year, weakened by tuberculosis contracted while in prison. William dies in Minneapolis in 1873.

The Goodridge presence in York resumes in 1891 when Glen J. Goodridge, Glenalvin's youngest son, returns to operate a barbershop. His mother, Rhoda, who also returned, remarries.

Her new husband is Abraham Rayno. Rhoda Goodridge Rayno died in 1903, and Glen J. Goodridge passed away in 1928.

Mother and son are buried in Lebanon Cemetery, North York.

The camera is turned on pioneer black American photographers, Wallace L. Goodridge and William O. Goodridge, seated, in this 1883 photo. The Goodridges were the sons of William C. Goodridge, the prominent York businessman. The Goodridge brothers operated a photo studio in East Saginaw, Mich. The studio, opened by another brother, Glenalvin, in York in 1847, operated for 75 years until Wallace L. Goodridge's death in 1922.

James Latimer, son of a wealthy York County family and later a county judge, poses for this Goodridge daguerreotype.

Dr. Charles H. Bressler, a prominent York County physician and ardent Republican, wrote this letter to his friend and political ally Pennsylvania Gov. Andrew G. Curtin urging the release of Glenalvin Goodridge, imprisoned after a rape conviction. 'There is not a man in our party but is satisfied that he never would have been convicted if he had been a white man and if he had been a Democrat,' he wrote. He also reminded the governor that some of the 'hardest Democrats' in York argued against the conviction. The letter contributed to Curtin's pardon of Goodridge in December 1864.

1863: York County
Blacks serve in Massachusetts unit

Four black soldiers from York County serve in the 54th Massachusetts Regiment.

George Ellender is wounded in the assault on Fort Wagner, S.C., that took the life of regiment commander Col. Robert Gould Shaw and is wounded a second time in Olustee, Fla.

Aaron Cummings is also wounded in Olustee, Fla. George Batson, a Peach Bottom farmer, and William Freeman, a Lower Chanceford farmer, also serve in the regiment.

One hundred and seventy-nine thousand black soldiers and 10,000 black sailors served in Union forces. Many were slaves only months, or days, before enlisting.

Thirty-eight thousand black soldiers and sailors lost their lives in combat or to disease, and 22 won the Medal of Honor, America's top award. The 54th Massachusetts Regiment is profiled in the 1989 movie "Glory."

1863: Warrington Township
Farmers shoot unknown man

Five Warrington Township men shoot a black man, probably a servant of an invading Confederate Army officer.

The unknown man had helped Confederates locate horses that farmers had hidden in the woods during the rebel invasion. When the Confederates departed, he had been left behind.

The party of farmers locates the servant and shoots him multiple times. They carry his body from the road and conceal him under some brush.

The Wells family from Wellsville hears of the incident, demands an inquest, and the five men, plus another prominent local man, are charged with murder.

Some of the men are jailed, but a grand jury "ignored the bill," and the judge dismisses the men.

A newspaper, bringing the incident to light more than 40 years later after one of the assailants came forward, claimed the incident was the county's only lynching.

1800s: York County
A view of Centre Hall

This stereograph, prepared for use in a stereoscope, shows Centre Hall, on the northwest angle of York's Centre Square, sometime before 1900. A stereoscope is an instrument with two eyepieces through which a pair of photographs, taken from slightly different angles, are viewed. When seen side by side, the single picture appears to have three dimensions or depth. William C. Goodridge constructed Centre Hall for $6,000 in 1847. Goodridge's barbershop, his toy shop and other enterprises occupied the first floor. At one time, the basement was occupied by an 'Oyster and Eating House.' Goodridge rented out the second floor to various businesses. The third floor was used for storage, and the Worth Infantry band practiced and gave concerts on the fourth floor, with its 10-foot ceiling. Glenalvin J. Goodridge used the top or fifth floor, with dormers and skylight, for his photography studio.

1864: Wrightsville
James Barton joins Army

James Barton answers the roll call at Camp William Penn in Philadelphia.

The 19-year-old Wrightsville man is ready to train as part of the 127th Regiment, United States Colored Troops. A life-threatening case of the measles soon brings his training to a halt. His face swells, closing his eyes to the point of blindness. His skin pales and becomes blotchy.

After two months in the hospital, the Army sends Barton home so that his family can care for him. "(H)e was home for more than a week... ," neighbor Josephine Elizabeth Brown said, "his face was swollen."

Despite his ill health, James Barton rejoins his unit. After the war ends, he travels with his regiment to Texas, where the soldiers are assigned to guard the Rio Grande against a suspected incursion by French troops.

He remains there until September 1865, when he travels to New Orleans and receives an honorable discharge. He receives discharge pay of $100 and owes the government $24.24 for his clothing.

His health broken by the war, Barton later fought a harsh battle for a full pension for Union veterans. Barton eventually received a monthly check of $6.

1865: York
Chief burgess sets protocol

Abraham Lincoln's funeral train passes through the county on its way to Springfield, Ill.

To prepare for its stop in York, Chief Burgess David Small issues an order that calls for:

1. All businesses to close after 4 p.m. on April 21 and remain closed as long as the body was in the state.
2. Military and citizens to assemble in York's Centre Square with the proces-

sion to march to the North Duke Street rail station. 3. The formation of a line at the station, extending toward Baltimore. "During the passing of the train the line will remain uncovered (with hats off)," the order stated. 4. Citizens to take their flags and "drapery of mourning" to Water Street for suspension along the buildings on the railroad line. 5. The tolling of bells while the body was within the borough limits. 6. For Col. J.A. Stahle to act as chief marshal.

Carrolus A. Miller, a Hanover native, pilots the train between Washington and Baltimore but is not at the helm when the train rides the Northern Central Railroad into York.

The train arrives late, stops where the tracks cross North Duke Street and stays about 10 minutes.

Six-year-old Henry C. Niles, later a York County judge, provides this recollection from his prime perch on the shoulders of his friend, John Joice, a young black waiter at the Washington House hotel: "The silent crowd made a way for York's floral expression of patriotism and grief, borne by Aquilla Howard, the tall negro butler of the Philip A. Small family. From John Joice's shoulder, I saw my mother, following Mrs. Samuel Small, pass into one car door and out the other."

1868: Washington, D.C.
York native elected bishop

Singleton T. Jones, born in Wrightsville in 1825, is elevated to the position of bishop of the A.M.E. Zion Church.

Jones

"Bishop Jones is one of our strong men," a denomination history stated, "he is distinguished as an energetic worker, as a pulpit orator, an eloquent and impressive preacher.... Long may he live to glorify God and bless his race."

1887: Wrightsville

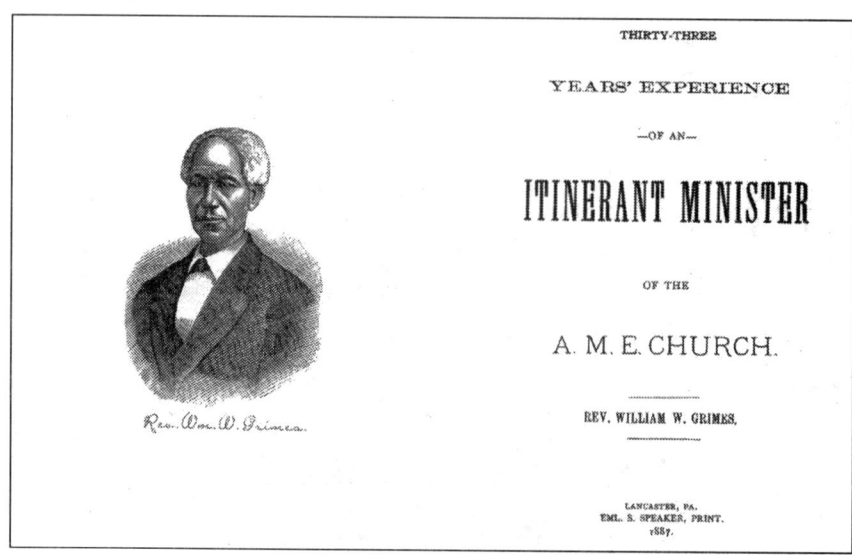

The Rev. William W. Grimes, who headed congregations in Wrightsville and York, left behind brief impressions of his long career at 18 different churches, primarily in Pennsylvania and New Jersey.

Itinerant pastor plants churches

The Rev. William W. Grimes publishes a booklet, "Thirty-three Years' Experience of an Itinerant Minister of the A.M.E. Church."

His short work details his ministry from the Smyrna Circuit in Delaware starting in 1855 to his pastorate in Wrightsville and York in 1887. The list of his 18 churches tells of the lives of many A.M.E. ministers, as they are reassigned by their conference every one or two years.

"I have received for the support of my family $78 for a year's salary," he wrote, "and when I received $150 I was getting a large salary."

The life of a minister produced high points — organizing new churches — and low points — difficult congregations.

"My prayers are, that you, my dear reader," he wrote, "may never have to pass through the hardships as I have done before you."

1869: Wrightsville
Camp meeting lasts two weeks

A gathering, described by a newspaper as a "colored camp meeting," begins in Ebert's woods about two miles from Wrightsville.

The meeting is large, and organizers set up about 20 tents. Attendance during the week lags, but Sunday draws a peak crowd.

"Religious services are conducted regularly with much zeal and animation," a newspaper reported. The gathering closes after two weeks of meetings.

1872: York
Former slave is at least 92

Jemima Jackson is one of the oldest women, if not the oldest, in the York community.

Early in life, she had been a slave belonging to Marylander Nathaniel Watts of Baltimore County. Her owner sought a Methodist pastorate but could not do so without manumitting his slaves. Once freed, Jackson and her sons came to York, later joined by her husband, Old Tom Jackson, as he was called.

Dates on her freedom papers make her 92 years old, but she recalls incidents that would make her older. She lives comfortably with her son, Tom, and keeps a small stock of candy for sale.

"She complains of rheumatism," a newspaper said, "but moves around quite lively and looks as if she might live another decade."

1880: York
Pastor becomes member of group

Silas Swallow, minister of First Methodist Episcopal Church, works for a rule change that would make John Price, his counterpart at the A.M.E. Zion Church, part of the York Ministerial Association.

When Swallow arrives in York in 1880, association rules state that one "no" vote can keep a minister from membership. Price withdraws his bid after learning that some association members would not approve his induction.

Swallow's efforts during his three years in York at present-day Asbury United Methodist Church results in a rule change to make all clergy ex-officio members.

The Rev. John H. Hector, Price's successor, thus becomes a member upon his arrival in York. This leads to the resignation of several association members.

1884: York
Swollen creek damages church

The Bethel A.M.E. Church in York sustains major losses when the flooding Codorus Creek overflows its banks.

The creek reaches the congregation's King Street building, causing $3,960 in damage.

"There is perhaps no other building on the street which suffered more from the ravaging flood, or left a more distressed state than this little church," an eyewitness commented. "…The altar, stove and carpet were among the debris which lined the street."

The church pays 25 cents each for 14 bushels of hair used to prepare the plaster.

Today, Bethel A.M.E. Church meets at 356 W. Princess St., York.

Late 1800s: York County
In the work force

A waiter stands ready at the York Collegiate Institute, a forerunner of York College, in this 1892 photograph. In the 1800s and early 1900s, black women seeking work in the white community often gained employment as nurses, cooks and household attendants. The black men found places in domestic and hotel service, contracting and common labor. Black men and women also formed their own businesses. Many were employed as barbers. A 1910 business directory of black-owned businesses listed 13 barber shops, four hairdressers and manicurists and one manufacturer of hair tonic. Other black-owned businesses included: billiard and pool rooms, two; cafe, one; caterer, two; phosphate dealer, one; hauling and draying, five; clerks, one; boarding and lodging, two; and restaurants, one.

1889: York County
Generations of Cupits

Merriman "Bob" Cupit, well-known York barber, dies at the age of 59.

Merriman Cupit

Cupit had followed the course of several blacks in York by studying to become a barber at the age of 10 in Baltimore. He operated several shops in York, taught school in Marietta for many years, and found time to serve the community. He was reportedly the first black to serve on a grand jury, acting as secretary of that body.

He was also selected to serve on a committee with U.S. lawmakers Salmon P. Chase and Charles Sumner to explore ways to improve life for 19th-century blacks.

"Merriman Cupit was in every sense a prominent person of his race and held numerous positions of honor and trust, all of which was acceptably filled," a newspaper reported.

Cupit and his wife, the former Jane Ann Johnson, had a son, Jehu, who followed his father as a barber. Jane Ann Johnson's mother, Julia Johnson, a pioneer among blacks in York, lived in the county for more than 80 years. She mothered her 16 children and then some.

As a domestic worker, she raised the children of the prominent Lewis family.

In addition to his barber shears, Jehu Cupit could also handle a pen. He writes a poetic, perhaps prophetic, description of York that focuses on the tottering Centre Square market sheds.

His sense of humor provides fodder for several newspaper articles.

A newspaper reporter visited his barbershop to gather stories from Cupit and his customers.

"Barber Cupit...can talk and it is a delight to sit in his shop across the (Codorus Creek) bridge and listen to the interesting tales he reels off when surrounded by a little company of auditors," the newspaper reported.

Cupit was a former editor as well as a barber. That's an odd combination but west-side people are known for their resourcefulness.

One west-side tradesman markets

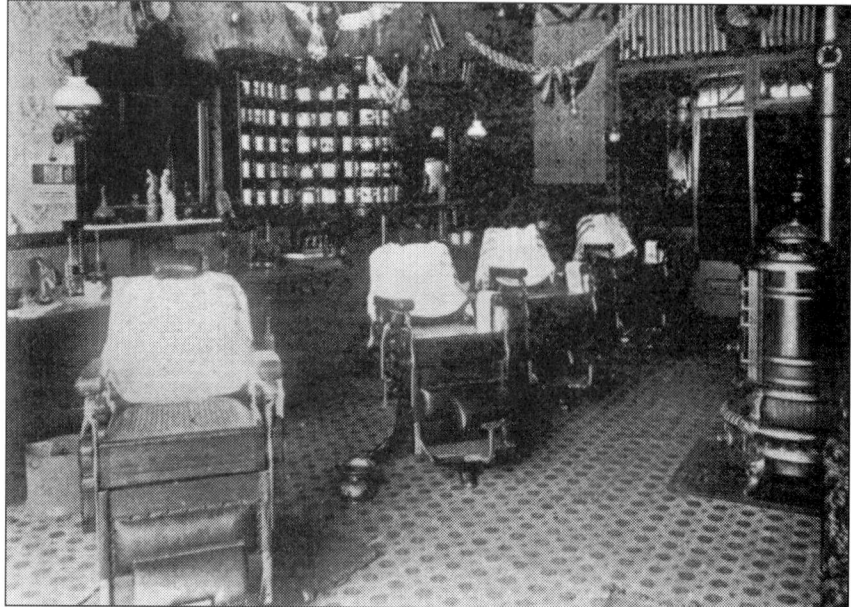
A book published as part of the 150th anniversary of York County in 1899 features a photo of Jehu Cupit's 'tonsorial parlors,' 228 W. Market St., York. Jehu Cupit was a member of a respected York County family. His father, Merriman 'Bob' Cupit, became well-known throughout Pennsylvania and America, developing a reputation for working for freedom for blacks. 'Having the advantages of little school education,' Merriman Cupit's obituary stated, 'through his inordinate love for books he acquired a storehouse of knowledge possessed by a few.' He passed on his love for learning to his son, who also was a noted member of the community.

oysters, coal oil, taffy and fertilizing material, the newspaper claimed.

Cupit edited a column in a now-defunct farm journal. He gathered his material by interviewing farmers at market. He, thus, discovered what interested them and advocated reforms of importance to tillers — better roads, equalization of taxes and longer school terms.

But the press of business caused him to give up his editorial pursuits.

A year later, Cupit — or Cupit's carbuncle — makes the news. The barber's nemesis for a week or more is about to fall off.

"Mr. Cupit is not loth to part with the stranger," a newspaper reported, "and will speed the parting guest with the aid of a variety of home-made poultices which friends have considerably recommended."

Jehu Cupit advertised his barbershop by issuing these cards bearing photographs of popular vehicles.

Late-1800s: York
'Ancient York'

Authorship of the poem "Ancient York" is attributed to Jehu Cupit, a well-known York barber. This work was found in the estate of Annie K. Buckingham, who died in the 1920s. The poem was written before 1887, when York's delapidated Centre Square market sheds were pulled down in the middle of the night. A controversy had erupted over whether the sheds should stay or go, and a band of men resolved the issue by hooking ropes to the shed poles and demolishing them. "Ancient York" was first published in The York Dispatch in 1927, signed by "Damon."

Old York, is builded, both high and wide,
On both sides of Codorus tide;
Which sweeps in dread majesty on
    toward the sea.
Bearing filth from the pulp-mills and city
    debris.

Old York is a place of wondorus renown,
As a cleanly and quiet, symmevilcal town;
And the fame of its industries, what'er they be,
Has spread to both worlds, and the isles of the sea.

Old York has buildings, both massive and light,
Well fitted to cause, e'en a critic delight;
Its court house and prison — from Havlland's hand,
Can contend for the palm, with the best in the land.

Then, there are the building, of later style,
Like the new City market — a wondorous pile;
Or the Mercantile building — so fair to behold,
Where Merchants and Lawyers, turn gas into gold.

But all the fine structures, which I might name,
Are distanced and made to look wordously tame;
When compared with that stately old pile
    in the square;
The Old Borough Market Sheds — offers beware.

Just who was the architect, nobody knows,
And nobody cares, except when it snows or rains,
Then the vagrants and dogs lay about,
On the butcher-blocks, whence fresh beef
    is dealt out.

That this is offensive, no one will deny,
And all world rejoice, it t'were blown high and dry;
But the wise Borough Fathers, say, T'is for our good,
And tell me my friend, if they don't know,
    who should.

The roofs of this structure, which first catch the eye,
Ave not every broad, nor yet very high;
They're covered with tin, and shaped like an egg,
To make them look handsome, they painted
    them red.

Iron columns, supports the dimiutive arch,
Under which the best Burghers of York, often march;
The floor is half brick, the other half boards,
And neath the later, the station house roads.

Tis said that a Roc, once, flew over the town,
And seeing the shed-roofs, began to come down;
It thought they were eggs, and ne'er found
    its mistake,
Till the tramps 'gan to cuss, and the rats got awake.

Strangers have said on coming to town,
That t'was Noah's old ark, turned upside down;
While a near-sighted drover, would straightway
    declare,
The Motter house stock sheds, were moved
    to the square.

That such things are undignified, each one perceives,
That the sheds are an eye-sore, each one believes;
But the wise Borough Fathers, say, t'is for our good
And tell me my friend, if they don't know
    who should?

Good Cyrus Diller in Hanover town,
Once dreamt, ohe Hanover sheds fell down;
When Lo As the darkness gave way to the dawn,
The Hanover sheds, were entirely gone.

If only some Yorker, who owns a good team,
Some night would have such a glorious dream;
I'm certain that when the glad morning would dawn,
The noxious old Roosts, would surely be gone.

— Attributed to Jehu Cupit

1890: York
No Small feats

The Rev. John B. Small, later Bishop Small, becomes pastor of the A.M.E. Zion Church on East King Street in York.

Small

Small, born in the British West Indies, filled the pulpit of many prominent churches before coming to York. His wife, Mary Jane Small, is also an ordained minister. John Small supports the temperance movement and is outspoken on other issues of the day. After his pastorate in York, he is named bishop in the A.M.E. Zion Church, a position of national prominence. The present-day Small Memorial A.M.E. Zion Church on South Queen Street in York bears his name.

Despite widespread travels in Africa, England and the West Indies, he apparently considered York home. When he died in 1905, he was buried in Lebanon Cemetery, North York.

1890: York
Minor league team calls York home

York fields a minor league baseball squad composed largely of the Cuban Giants, an early all-black professional team. J. Monroe Kreiter brings the York Monarchs to town.

The team and community seem to have a close relationship. When the first-place team returns to town after a road trip, about 2,000 fans greet the players at the train station. The Spring Garden Band leads the team in a parade that ends at Centre Square.

"Let the boys keep up the good work, and they will have friends in York who will not let them go begging," a newspaper said.

As the season progresses, Kreiter decides to move the team to Harrisburg.

"We will play under the name of the Colored Monarchs...from the historic town of York," he said.

c. 1890: Lower Chanceford Twp.
Church organizes in rural township

A meeting place for Chanceford A.M.E. Zion Church, sometimes called Stephenson Chapel, is listed on the tax rolls in the 1890s.

Church members include the Young, Wilson, Berry, Dorsey, Lee, Jefferson, Fells, Wallace, Barton, Hopkins and Saulsbury families. Many of these families move to York but worship at Chanceford.

The congregation organizes camp meetings the last two Sundays in July. A stove is set up under trees. A Thanksgiving meal is served in the fall when seats are taken out of the church to accommodate those gathered. The Rev. Lewis H. Jiles is the last pastor to serve the Chanceford and Fawn churches.

Today, the cemetery remains, but the log building is gone.

1894: York
Black Republicans seek an identity

A black Republican club is reportedly forming in York, but no one shows at the announced meeting.

John F. Noble, Jehu G. Cupit, Policeman Diggs and other prominent black Republicans do not know where the report came from.

Noble, a leader of York blacks in the Garfield-Hancock presidential race, thinks an organization of black Republicans makes sense.

"There are a great many young men among our people who are intelligent and naturally ambitious," he told a newspaper. "They consequently feel the need for such an organization and would be identified with any movement having for its end the formation of a club. I think, by all means, we should have such a club."

1895: York
G.A.R. remembers Civil War dead

The David E. Small Post 369, G.A.R., completes Memorial Day arrangements to commemorate the dead in Lebanon Cemetery on the 30th anniversary of the ending of the Civil War.

Cyrus Johnson would lead the black Grand Army of the Republic procession, which plans to assemble at the Smallwood School on Water Street for its walk to the North York cemetery.

The Metropolitan Band would lead the march, followed by the drum corps, a hearse with flowers, carriage with speakers, children, post members and participating organizations.

Children would carry flags supplied at the school. The Christian Endeavor Flower Committee would bring flowers, and the call goes out for all marching to bring some along.

The Rev. J. H. Hector is the scheduled orator at the cemetery.

1897: York
Goodridge house bought

Noted architect Reinhardt Dempwolf purchases a house at 123 E. Philadelphia St., previously owned by William C. Goodridge.

Goodridge hid runaway slaves in the cellar and in pits in his back yard. Dempwolf refurbishes the house and changes its facade. It later falls into disrepair until restored in the mid-1990s.

1901: York
Last person laid to rest in cemetery

Mary Baptist, said to be the oldest black woman in York, dies in her South Water Street home and is buried in the Moravian Cemetery, west of the intersection of Princess and Water streets.

At the time of her death, the 98-year-old is the only black person who was a member of the Moravian Church in York. She is the last person to be buried in the Moravian Cemetery, located near the church's early buildings. Years earlier, the congregation moved to its present-day North Duke Street building, and the cemetery fell into neglect.

In 1908, the bodies of Baptist and others interred in the old cemetery were moved. Baptist's body was moved to Lebanon Cemetery in North York and others to Prospect Hill Cemetery.

In 1919, the church leased the former cemetery site to the city and it was used as a playground for black children.

1903: York
Pitcher throws perfect game

The Cuban X-Giants, a team made up of former Cuban Giants players, makes a stop in York for a three-game series against York's Penn Park Athletic Club. The barnstorming Negro League players handle the local team roughly.

In one game, the X-Giants' Danny McClellan pitches a perfect game before a crowd of 300 people. A newspaper called McClellan's performance in retiring all 27 Penn Park batters the greatest exhibition of pitching ever seen in York.

Another newspaper carried the story with the headline, "Oh Me! Oh My! Alack! We Didn't Get a Smack!

"Thus, she carried the entire nine acts, and when her thirst for blood had finally been satisfied," the newspaper said in casting the game story as if it were a play, "the carcasses of 27 suckers were hauled off to the fertilizer generator, and not a speck of her disguise had been ruffled by the clubs of her assailants."

1905: York County
Servant status called a killer

Indentured servanthood long has been abolished, but its effect is still felt.

William Butler was bound, or indentured, to a master for seven years early in life. One winter, his master took him to northern Pennsylvania to drag logs to the river. His feet froze, and he became crippled.

Butler later worked for York lawyer John Evans and banker Eli Lewis. Butler, a black man who could not read or write, did not know when he was born. Some estimate that he is more than 100 years old when he dies in 1905, and he had just resigned as janitor of the Smallwood School.

Butler suffered gangrene in his feet, which contributed to his death. "It was one of the ironies of fate," a newspaper reported, "that his death was finally due to the cruelty of the master of many years ago."

Early 20th century
Everyday life

A well-dressed man guides a team of horses pulling a Conewago Gas Co. float in a Hanover parade early in the 20th century.

1905: York
Black woman gains work in factory

Twenty-year-old Ethel Cowles gains employment in a sewing factory, believed to be the only black woman holding a skilled job in a York manufacturing plant.

Cowles had worked at the Ebenheimer and Obendorff shirt factory, corner of Howard and Newton avenues, for three years.

"...(S)he is rated among the valued and well paid employes of the plant," a newspaper reported.

She gains employment when a white woman seamstress became ill and recommended Cowles, daughter of the late Jesse Sumner Cowles, as her substitute.

When the ill woman recovered, the plant superintendent, impressed with Cowles, decided to retain her, "providing the other employes were not incuded to draw the color line," the newspaper stated.

After a factory-wide canvass, no one objects to Cowles' regular employment.

The newspaper checked if other black women were so employed in York and concluded Cowles was the only skilled worker. The city's black population totalled 3,000, the newspaper stated.

1907: York
Prominent York resident dies

Alexander McKinney, a 79-year-old former slave, dies at his York home.

McKinney had been born on a plantation near Shepardstown, Va., in 1828 and worked there until 1863.

When Confederate troops

approached the plantation, his master freed him.

McKinney and his wife, the former Sarah Sands, came to York, where he achieved prominence in the black community.

At the time of his death, he served as past most noble father, Hand-in-Hand Lodge, Grand United Order of Odd Fellows.

1908: York
Church leader passes away

Greenberry S. Robinson, described as the leading hairdresser in York for many years, passes away.

The York native, whose age was about 70 years old, held all the offices in the East King Street A.M.E. Zion Church a layman could fill.

He served as a cook in the Civil War.

"The older citizens knew him favorably well," his obituary said, "for he was one of the most popular colored men in York."

1913: York
Noted judge speaks in York

Before Black History Month and Martin Luther King Jr.'s birthday, Jan. 1 is observed as a time to consider the accomplishments of blacks and their strides toward freedom.

The Emancipation Proclamation became effective on Jan. 1, 1863, freeing slaves in the Southern states. Fifty years later, blacks and whites brave the winter cold in York to fill the East King Street A.M.E. Zion Church.

They are eager to hear Robert H. Terrell, America's first black federal judge, speak at the Emancipation Day jubilee. Before Terrell speaks, a young black choir sings "The Star-Spangled Banner" with such patriotic emotion, according to one historian, "that there was hardly a dry eye in the audience."

Then Terrell speaks: "Since then (1863), we have steadily made significant strides toward gaining our political, economic and intellectual freedom. And this is because America, of all countries, is most free. And because of this freedom, we blacks have made advancement in numerous ways since 1863."

1913: York

In the late 1800s and early 1900s, Small Memorial A.M.E. Zion, Bethel A.M.E., Faith Presbyterian and Shiloh Baptist were York's four most visible black churches. Shiloh Baptist dated back to the 1880s. Here, the Rev. Richard J. Manning is shown with Shiloh Baptist's Young People Choir from a later period —1962. First row, from left: Pearl Keenheel, director; Carol Carter; Lawrence Dickson; Beatrice Williams; Maria Dickson; Carole Manning; Katherine Orr, president; Margie Orr; and Clarence Peterson. Second row, from left: Howard Guion; Madel Carter; the Rev. Manning; Betty Tyler; and Russell Dorm Jr.

New building sports a baptistery

Elizabeth Laws is the first member of Shiloh Baptist Church to undergo baptism in the font in the church's new building.

Church records indicate that the baptistery was a draw. People came from miles around to witness immersions in the new font.

Before the church with baptistery was built on a triangular site at Edgar and Princess streets, the baptisms were performed at several locations: First Baptist Church in Columbia; the Vander Avenue Church of God, a white congregation; and the stream flowing near American Chain and Cable Co.

The church is moved, baptistery and all, four years later. Workers place the structure on rollers and relocate it to 617 E. Princess St., York.

Manning   Jones

The Rev. Richard J. Manning came to York in 1952 from Baltimore to take over the pastorate of Shiloh Baptist Church from longtime minister William E. Jones. Jones had served in the pulpit for 35 years. When Jones came to York from Harrisburg, the doors of the church were closed. He worked to build up the congregation and later constructed a new building. '...(H)e weathered numerous stormy seas with the help of various faithful members...,' a church history observes. Shiloh Baptist continued to thrive under Manning.

1914: York County
Suffragists tour York County

Anna Dill Gamble agrees to lead the fight to persuade political leaders and other men to support the right of women to vote.

"...I congratulate you all on the fine spirit with which the skirmish line of your forces presses forward. ...To me it looks as irresistible as that force of which it was once said, 'You might as well attempt to dam the Nile with bulrushes,'" Robert Bair of York wrote Gamble.

The campaign features a county tour of a large Suffrage or Women's

Liberty Bell, designed to inspire support for the cause. The day before voters decide the suffrage question in Pennsylvania in 1915, Dr. George W. Bowles, a leader in the black community, introduces Mrs. Paul Lawrence Dunbar at a pro-suffrage rally.

Mrs. Dunbar, widow of the noted black poet, argues that women should have the right to vote because they are increasingly working outside the home, paying taxes and want to look "personally after the things that effect their own lives." Men in the county defeat the suffrage amendment by an 11,284 to 5,103 vote.

"I saw scores of men taken into the polls and voted like sheep," Gamble commented. "If all these men couldn't read and write, then the male illiteracy in York must be enormous. They had better let some women in who won't need so much assistance."

The Nile, indeed, could not be dammed, and American women voted for the first time five years later.

1918: France
York soldier killed in Europe

Pvt. George Woods, a black soldier from York and member of the 41st Machine Gun Battalion, is killed somewhere in France in World War I.

Wood, the son of Anna Woods and a resident of 428 E. King St., leaves home for Camp Lee, Va., in early 1918.

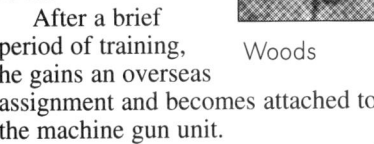
Woods

After a brief period of training, he gains an overseas assignment and becomes attached to the machine gun unit.

He is killed in September, one of 195 York County residents to die in the war.

1922: York
Young women's club gains charter

York County Court grants the Emergency Girls' Club, a group organized by Ida Grayson and Helen L. Thackston, a charter to operate as a nonprofit organization.

The club is dedicated to providing recreational, social, religious and educational facilities for maturing black girls and young women. In its early years, the club meets in the North Duke Street home of Mary Barton, doing war work to support the Negro branch of the American Red Cross.

Despite these high goals, the organization's quest for a charter meets opposition that lasts for a year. The purchase of a house at 145 W. Princess St. attracts opposition led by pastors George S. Albright and I.S. Lee. They said the club had generated so many complaints that a city police officer was stationed in the area to preserve order, and the organization generally lowered the morals of the community.

Bootlegging, noise and disorderliness were among the complaints.

After a hearing, the court grants

1919: Cly

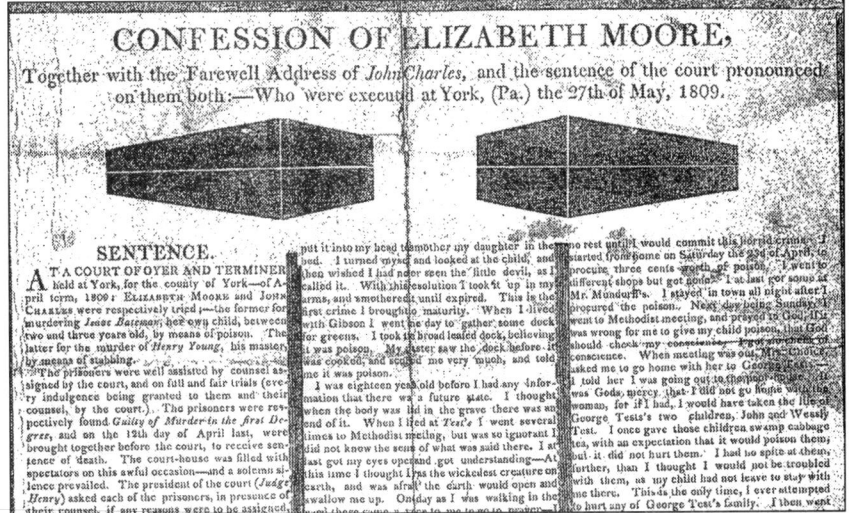

The confessions of Elizabeth Moore and John Charles, awaiting death by hanging after being found guilty in York County Court, were published in 1809.

Executions centralized

Curtis Sipple, alias Robert E. Hicks, kills co-workers Gabriel Perrachia and James Critchlow with a metal bar as part of a robbery plan in Cly in 1919.

For his crime, Sipple, a 19-year-old white man, is executed in the electric chair at Rockview State Prison. Pennsylvania centralized its executions at Rockview in 1915. Before that, executions took place, often publicly, in counties where the crimes were committed.

Several men and women were hanged in York County between 1749 and 1915.

One of the most noteworthy involved Elizabeth Moore, a runaway slave, who was hanged in 1809 for poisoning her 2-year-old son, Isaac Bateman. Moore confessed to committing the crime so the boy could join his infant sister in heaven. Moore also admitted she had smothered her young daughter.

Her execution was delayed after she became pregnant in jail and bore a child. Her prosecution coincided with that of John Charles, a French Creole man convicted of stabbing his master, Henry Young. Both Moore and Charles were sentenced to death by hanging on the same day before a packed courthouse.

Today, 11 men from York County sit on death row. Six are white: James W. Begley, Karl Stephenson Chambers, Kevin Brian Dowling, Hubert Lester Michael Jr., John Amos Small and Mark Newton Spotz. Four are black: James Henry Carpenter, Daniel Jacobs, Charles Malloy and Paul Gamboa-Taylor; and one is Hispanic: Milton Montalvo.

the charter. Interest diminished after 1935, and the club disbanded in 1959. Construction of the Park Lane Plaza parking facility, opposite William Penn High School, meant an end to the old club.

Other clubs have been part of the black community over the years.

The Royal Whist Society formed in 1915. This men's club met every Saturday night to play Whist, a forerunner of bridge.

William Myers earned the designation "Whist Society Mogul" as one of the best players in this elite club. The club disbanded in 1965.

At the time of race riots in York in 1969, the 310 Club was formed to provide recreational opportunities for black youth. The club met in the former York News Agency building for about a year.

Today, the Northeast Social Club remains visible. The organization, which started in the late 1970s, now includes 25 men who grew up in "Parkway," the public housing development on York's Parkway Boulevard.

In 2001, the club honored the women who helped raise them with a dinner, fashion show and dance at the Valencia Ballroom.

1927: York
Myers begins long career at hotel

The newly opened The Yorktowne Hotel needs a bell captain, and its manager finds a long-lasting one at the Penn Hotel on North George Street.

William E. Myers arrives at the Yorktowne in 1927, joined over the years by members of his family.

Myers

One of William Myers' uncles, Frank Charms, served as maitre d'. Another uncle, Davie Myers, was a cook. Uncles Milton Myers and Samuel Grimes served as bellmen. Myers' wife ran the elevator for several years. His son, Bill, worked part-time in the garage. Myers' granddaughter, Linda, worked in the accounting office.

Myers played a part in a daily ritual at the Yorktowne. Two bellmen and a bell captain worked in two shifts. At 6 p.m., the shifts changed, and the bellmen paraded around three stops — the bellman's bench in the lobby and the two entrances. A trio on the mezzanine supplied the music. At each station, the evening bellman dropped out to replace his day counterpart.

Evening had begun.

"When William Myers retired in 1977," a hotel history states, "his career with the hotel was distinguished not only as the longest in hotel records, but also among the finest."

1928: York
Church gains new minister

The Rev. Thomas E. Montouth, a voice for civil rights in York for decades, takes over the pastorate of Faith Presbyterian Church.

Within three years, the minister becomes a charter member of the Crispus Attucks Association. He serves on its board for years.

Montouth

He also is a leader in the local branch of the National Association for the Advancement of Colored People.

The Faith Presbyterian congregation had formed in June 1894 and moved into its North Duke Street building later that year. The Rev. E. W. Coberth was the founding minister.

1929: North York
Klan Konklave finds a home

North York's chief burgess, council members and playground association members ride in two cars leading a parade. Five hundred marchers in full uniform follow.

Participants end up in the community playground, where 5,000 people observe an induction ceremony for 51 men, 23 women and 13 junior candidates dressed in full regalia.

The last evening of the three-day convention ends with the firing of one 60-foot cross and 15 crosses, 15-feet high. The state Konklave of the Ku Klux Klan in Pennsylvania concludes.

The Klan displays a decided anti-Catholic bent in these days.

York is a hotbed of Klan activity and home to a "great titan," a state leader in the Ku Klux Klan movement. Earlier in the decade, York counts the sixth-largest lodge in the state with 1,518 members.

Churches often play host to Klan activities. About 100 Klanswomen attend Sunday evening services at a Dallastown church in 1926. The women assemble in the west end of town and march to the church in hoods and gowns.

A Dover-area church, constructed in 1927, still displays a stained glass window donated by the KKK.

In the 1990s, York County remained an area of white supremacist activity. A scholar noted that rightists in York are divided between overt Nazis and patriotic ultraconservatives. Klan activists in contemporary Pennsylvania ostensibly concern themselves with such mainstream issues as opposition to abortion, drugs and pornography.

1931: York
Crispus Attucks gets its start

The Crispus Attucks Community Center is founded in York as a social and recreational facility for the black community.

Crispus Attucks, believed to be the son of an African man and Nantucket Indian woman, was the first person to die in the American Revolution. He was one of five people killed in the Boston Massacre in 1770.

The old York Hospital serves as an early center site.

The center moves to the former St. Luke's Lutheran Church on East Maple Street in 1944.

Helen L. Thackston was a constant at the center from its opening until 1964. She served as director of the Crispus Attucks preschool program from its opening until 1964.

Helen Thackston Memorial Park in York is named after this city native.

1920s-1930s: New Freedom
North on the York County Express

Weary passengers, long on the train from the Deep South, roll along on the Northern Central Railroad line from Baltimore.

They cross the invisible Mason-Dixon Line, pass New Freedom, Glen Rock and a number of smaller stations, and enter the dark Howard Tunnel before reaching their destination, York. They are among the migration of blacks moving from agrarian Bamberg, S.C., to a York County that is growing in industrial might.

Many Bambergers are the descendants of Isaac S. and Josephine Grayson Nimmons. Of the Nimmons' 14 children, seven settled in York or gave birth to children who later came here.

The Bambergers are just part of thousands who arrive in York County from 1880 to 1930, with 1905 as the mid-point. The census in York climbed from 13,940 in 1880 to 55,254 in 1930, and during this period, the county population almost doubles.

These are vintage years of the county's industrial growth. P.H. Glatfelter leads his paper company into black ink and then strengthens York Manufacturing Company, now York International. A.B. Farquhar captains his farm machinery business to international renown. York is known worldwide for its safes, pianos, chains, cigars, automobiles, wallpaper and false teeth.

Such industrial might attracts the Nimmons family, Italians, Greeks and others of backgrounds different than the German, English and Scotch-Irish families that dominate the county.

Today, scores count themselves as descendants of the Nimmonses. County residents of African-American descent named (or had a forebear named) Green, Jones, Kearse, Orr, Saxon or Varnes could be descendants of the Nimmonses.

Economic expansion after World War I meant a call for jobs in York and other industry-rich cities. This call reached into the Deep South, to places like Bamberg, S.C., where land was becoming scarce. Solomon Washington, above, farms the family homestead in Bamberg in 1996. Many Bambergers came to York to stay. Some, like Washington, returned. 'It (York) was a stone's throw from Baltimore, which was a major rail link to the North,' Charles Orr, whose family has Bamberg roots, recalled. 'York was virtually a straight line to better housing; better schools; no rigid segregation laws; a pace of life similar to 'down home,' a straight line to jobs and opportunity.'

The Northern Central Railroad Station in New Freedom, just north of the Mason-Dixon Line, greeted travelers from the South as they headed via rail for industrial jobs in York.

This diorama, at the York County Heritage Trust's Historical Society Museum, shows the homestead of the Isaac S. Nimmons family in Bamberg, S.C., about the year 1900.

1931: York
School district opens buildings

An influx of black families from the South to York causes construction of two elementary schools in the York City School District.

A new Smallwood School on Pershing Avenue is built near the old school building. A building, called the Aquilla Howard School, is constructed on East King Street. At the Smallwood School dedication in which Supt. Arthur W. Ferguson presided, the Rev. John T. Colbert gave the address.

Others participating in the dedication program that day: the Rev. Thomas E. Montouth gave the invocation; Penn Hotel Singers, directed by Reginald Dennis, performed "Old Man River" and "Water Boy"; the Men's Brotherhood, with Dennis also directing, presented a flag; Henry W. Hopewell, Smallwood principal, accepted the banner; and the Rev. J. Walter Morgan gave the benediction. The Smallwood work cost about $100,000.

The Aquilla Howard School, named after an early black leader of York, stands on East King Street. The school was built in 1931 to accommodate a growing number of blacks from the South arriving in industrial York. The school was used for special classes for students with learning disabilities starting in the 1956-57 school year. As part of Supt. Arthur W. Ferguson's realignment, the Duke Street School, oldest in the district, would no longer house special-needs students and would be used for warehouse purposes. The Aquilla Howard School was sold in 1962 and later demolished.

The Smallwood School on Pershing Avenue served as a social center for the black community. Above, the York Recreation Commission's Winter 1954 indoor play program kicks off at the school. The building was used as a language arts laboratory after desegregation was ordered in 1954 and later demolished to make way for a William Penn High School expansion.

Smallwood School, an elementary school for black children, was established in 1892. James Stewart was principal and Daisy Butler and Ella J. Robinson, teachers, in the 1893-94 year. Above, a new Smallwood School, constructed in 1931, stands near William Penn High School.

This undated photo shows perhaps all the students at Smallwood School.

1933: York
Civil War veteran dies

Joseph J. Howard, whose obituary said he was the last of the black Civil War veterans in York, dies at the age of 90 in 1933.

Howard had served in the Fifth Regiment, Massachusetts Cavalry.

Many other soldiers from York County served in Negro troops, including Levi Taylor of Wrightsville, a 12-year-old band boy, who died in the 1940s.

Some are buried in southeastern York County or lived there for many years: J. T. Young, George Barton, John H. Barton, James Jefferson, Stephen Barton, Nathaniel Bones, William E. Bones, Charles Davis, John T. Stephenson and Richard Lee.

1933: York County
Suicides, thefts mark Depression

More than 23,500 county residents are jobless as unemployment during the Great Depression reaches its peak.

"Business bankruptcies were more frequent," one history stated. "People stole more. Food thefts from farms were especially high. Banks continued to go under — in Dillsburg and Hallam. June, the traditional month for marriages, saw license applications drop off precipitously."

A shoeless Yorker smashes a $300 shoe store window to steal a pair of $3.95 boots. A large shantytown grows west of York, and its occupants are ordered to leave.

"Men who had worked hard all their lives and had never been forced to accept charity grew hopeless walking the streets looking for nonexistent jobs," one history stated. The state sets up a commissary, and recipients carry handouts home in burlap bags draped over their shoulders.

"It was a degrading process to be forced to parade one's poverty in public, most agreed, but it was better than starvation," the history said.

Women and minorities are among the worst-hit victims. Women faint while waiting in long bread lines. The York School Board notifies married female teachers that they can expect to be laid off to make room for unemployed men.

1931: York
Everyday life

A Lincoln impersonator is flanked by two aging Civil War veterans. The black veteran is thought to be John Aquilla Wilson, known as 'Quil,' of Fawn Township. He enlisted in the Negro troops, Company B, 32nd Regiment, Volunteer Infantry, in 1864. Wilson died at the age of 101.

Newspapers report that women, as well as men, are committing suicide over financial losses. Women hoboes are seen for the first time riding trains through York.

A black man drowns in Codorus Creek trying to salvage driftwood to sell. Dr. George W. Bowles, York physician, urges fellow blacks not to be timid in bread lines at the York County Home.

Blacks should learn their rights and make sure they get their fair share of welfare, he said.

Bowles

Some blacks who came to York in the 1920s ask county government to pay their fare back to the South.

1936: Fawn Township
Man sustains first serious injury

John Aquilla Wilson, known as "Quil," of Fawn Township breaks his leg in a fall from his porch, the first serious injury of his long life.

The snow-covered roads keep away medical help for the 95-year-old veteran of the Civil War's Negro troops until the next morning. The doctor orders Wilson to the hospital after seeing how badly his leg is broken.

"The neighbors, who gathered to see him being hauled away with so little pomp, were saddened," a newspaper said, "They felt that the same ambulance that took him away would soon be bringing his body home."

Seven weeks later, he returns from York Hospital. Before the summer is over, he is riding horseback with the same abandon as ever.

Wilson lived to be 101 and is buried in the Fawn A.M.E. Cemetery.

1937: York
Black athletes shine nationally

Paul E. Stephens of York retires after playing shortstop for the Pittsburgh Crawfords and several other Negro league teams in a career that started in 1921.

Other black athletes to play professionally include: Chris Doleman, Andre Powell, Omar Brown and Woody Bennett, who played in the NFL. Brad Carr and Tim Kearse played in the Canadian Football League.

Tremitiere

Chantel Tremitiere, a William Penn High School grad, was a starting point guard for the Sacramento Monarchs in the Women's National Basketball Association.

Tyrone Doleman, formerly of William Penn High School, played for the Harlem Globetrotters.

1938: York
Housing for poor top issue

A newspaper photograph shows a single faucet and sink used in a home for cooking, bathing and washing the family clothing.

When the pan beneath the sink's drain becomes full, its contents must be thrown out the door. Another photo shows a shack located next to an ash pile between King Street and Mason Alley.

The York County Industrial Union Council invites housing experts to the area to highlight the need for low-income residences. The movement could result in the formation of a housing authority.

The Depression slows building of all structures, the union notes, but housing for the low-income is never a priority even during the best of times.

"In many cases the plumbing is outside," the newspaper reported. "The outside toilet has not disappeared, the sloping roof of a certain shaped two by four in the backyard completes the picture... ."

1940: York
Well-known barber passes away

William Thomas Jones, who served as a barber in York into his 80s, dies from complications of a number of diseases.

Jones owned barbershops for years at 158 N. George St. and 17 East Charles Alley, his residence. He cut hair until only a year before his death, when he entered the York County home.

Jones, born near Cockeysville, Md., was also known for his feats as a young prizefighter. The black fighter was a familiar sight in the Old York Opera House ring.

1919-1945: York County
Scouts lodge at Camp Ganoga

Camp Ganoga, purchased in 1919, is the York-Adams Area Boy Scout Council's first full-time camp in York County, using permanently constructed buildings. It was located across the Big Conewago Creek near Strinestown, reachable by an old iron bridge. Ganoga, an Indian word for 'by the water,' was difficult to reach from York. Campers would take the trolley to Conewago Heights, then hike 3-1/2 miles to Ganoga. The council outgrew the camp, and it closed in 1945. Camping activities shifted to Camp Tuckahoe in 1948. Here, a group of scouts sits at the Camp Ganoga waterfront in 1939. Girl Scouting was popular among black girls in York as well.

This unidentified man is perhaps a camp cook.

These Scouts celebrate what appears to be a victory in some competition.

Chapter III: 1941-2002
While Johnny marches, York plans and Rosie rivets

Pfc. Charles E. Williams is killed in Italy as the Allies advance toward Germany. He had entered the service in 1941. An American Legion post on York's Princess Street is named in his honor.

B*usinessmen with briefcases meet in a smoke-filled room to look over lists of subcontractors who can handle work from the latest government war contracts. The York Plan is working, organizing workers, machinery and material to better the Allied cause in World War II and to bring home government contracts to York County. Those behind the York Plan adopt the motto: "To do what we can with what we have."*

With the brass working to bring in contracts and fighting men dug into trenches in Europe and the Pacific islands, women operate lathes, drills and punches in county manufacturing plants.

At home and abroad, the county stands like a Sherman tank behind war efforts.

Off the coast of Greenland, an enemy torpedo strikes the S.S. Dorchester. The ship is going down, and lifeboats and life belts are limited. Four chaplains, including York County's Rabbi Alexander Goode, give up their life belts — and their lives — so others can live.

In Italy, Pfc. Charles E. Williams is killed in action, less than two months before the war ends. He was one of six York County brothers, sons of Henry H. and Geraldine Williams, serving in the armed forces during the war. In southern France, Gen. Jacob L. Devers leads the Allied invasion. The York native returns to his hometown after the war with a coveted fourth star. York County pays a stiff price in the war. Five hundred and seventy county residents are killed. Peace is declared in 1945, and surviving county residents, having now seen the world, come marching home again eager to get on with their lives.

1942: York
In the work force

For decades, blacks served as laborers on construction crews working around York. Above, a crew from Henry E. Barton, a Philadelphia contractor, paves North George Street in North York in 1921.

Workers stand behind a coffer dam to work on the foundation of the Pennsylvania Railroad bridge in York. Their work is part of the U.S. Army Corps of Engineers' Codorus Creek Channel Improvements in 1942. Codorus Creek work in the Depression era had the dual purpose of providing jobs and enlarging the channel through York. The city was devastated in the flood of 1933 and damaged by another flood in 1936. The floods of 1933 and 1972 particularly affected many blacks, who often lived in houses near the creek.

This poster promotes a concert by noted black singers, Marian Anderson and Roland W. Hayes, in 1941. An audience at the William Penn High School auditorium warmly received the duo.

1941: York
Anderson, Hayes sing to encores

Contralto Marian Anderson and tenor Roland W. Hayes, billed as the foremost black singers in America, captivate an audience of about 600 people in the William Penn High School auditorium.

The singers' repertoire ranges from Negro ballads and spirituals to interpretations of French and Italian compositions. They perform Muldach's "The Passage Bird's Farewell" as their closing number.

A newspaper reported that the audience of white and black music lovers provided equal rounds of applause and requested numerous encores. Two years earlier, the Daughters of the American Revolution had denied Anderson permission to sing in Constitution Hall in Washington, D.C., because of her race. The Philadelphia native sang instead at the Lincoln Memorial before 75,000 people.

Conductor Arturo Toscanini praised Anderson's voice as one "heard once in a hundred years."

1941: York
School athletes cross race lines

York's elementary schools are mostly segregated, but athletes from both black and white schools compete against each other on the field.

Boy and girl teams from the Smallwood School win the annual

elementary school track and field meet staged at Small Athletic Field. Doris Blauser, whom a newspaper described as a "comely miss from Roosevelt school," is the meet's outstanding performer with two first places and a tie for top honors in a third event.

A list of the competing schools gives a glimpse at the schools in York: Smallwood, Ridge, Franklin, Noell, Pine, Roosevelt, Aquilla Howard, McKinley, Jefferson, Central, Garfield, Stevens and Hartley.

1941: York
Krupa's 'rumpus' points out racism

Gene Krupa and his band, fresh from a Thanksgiving concert at the Valencia Ballroom, stop into Bury's Restaurant on North George Street for a meal.

Restaurant employees refuse to serve two blacks — one musician in the famous drummer's orchestra and the other a stagehand. Krupa refuses to leave and, with profanity mixed in, states, "The best thing you can do is shut your mouth or we'll show you how to run this town."

A police officer steps in, believing the conversation was at the "rumpus" stage. He arrests Krupa on disorderly conduct charges, and the bandleader posts a $10 bond for his appearance in police court.

Krupa, then on to his next gig, does not appear, and Mayor Harry B. Anstine declares Krupa forfeited $10 to the city.

"When we get down south where they have 'Jim Crow' laws, (Trumpeter Roy) Eldridge and Waverly Ivey, the property man, who is also colored, expect these things, but not in Pennsylvania," Krupa told a newspaper. "We have made at least ten stops in Pennsylvania in the last month and never had any trouble until we ran up against that hamburger joint in York and that police officer."

Representing gold, silver and blue star war mothers, these women unveil a memorial on Penn Common on Veterans Day, 1946. From left, Lizzie Doll, gold star mother; Mrs. McKinley Harley, blue star mother; and Bessie E. Lloyd, silver star mother, are part of the ceremony. In those war years, the gold star hung in windows of families who had a member killed in action. Blue stars were awarded to families with a member in the service. Silver stars were awarded to families with a member who showed gallantry in action.

1942: Wrightsville
Civil War vet dies at advanced age

George W. Watson, the last surviving Civil War veteran in Wrightsville, dies at the age of 96.

Watson claimed to be born in 1841. His discharge papers from the U.S. Army after the Civil War would have made him 96.

His unit in the United States Colored Troops was present at Lee's surrender at Appomattox Court House, Va. His regiment was ordered to Washington, D.C., upon the death of Abraham Lincoln.

After the war, he worked in Marietta, Lancaster County, before moving across the river to Wrightsville where he labored in the stone quarries. He also worked as a boatman on the canals running from the Chesapeake Bay to Wrightsville and points north and east.

In 1941, Watson served as chief marshal at Wrightsville Memorial Day exercises. Failing health kept him from participating in 1942.

1942: York
Future scientist enters service

Henry C. Orr enters the service after graduation from William Penn High School. He serves with the 476th Amphibious Truck Company that served with distinction in the battle for Iwo Jima.

He later receives a Purple Heart for wounds sustained as part of the all-black unit in the Pacific Theater.

Orr

Orr went on to a career as a widely published scientist, earning his Ph.D. in biochemistry from George Washington University in 1967. He retired from the National Institutes of Health and was previously employed by the Food and Drug Administration.

He is one of the first black graduates from William Penn High School to hold a doctorate.

1940s: York County
Racial discrimination

York Gazette and Daily cartoonist Walt Partymiller shows a derailed Freedom Train. The train, carrying America's documents of liberty, stopped in York as part of a national tour in 1948. The newspaper contrasted the ideals of the documents with recent acts of racial discrimination in York: Council had closed the city-run pool rather than allow blacks the opportunity to swim there, and a York restaurant had refused service to a black veteran.

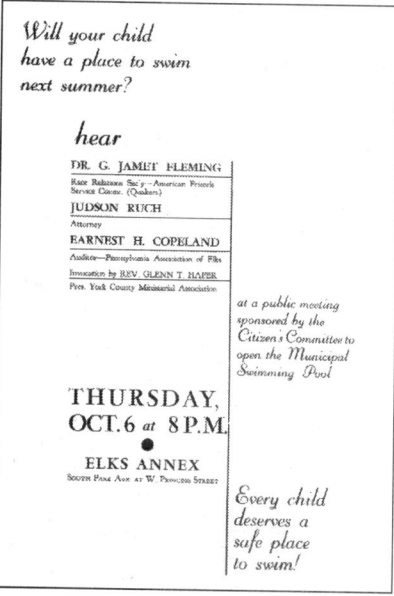

An advertisement calls for a meeting of those interested in opening the municipal pool to blacks. The Boys Club later operated the pool, and swimmers of all races eventually were allowed to swim there.

Here, a pair of swimmers in the 1990s enjoy the cool water at the Farquhar Park pool, as it's known today.

1944: Fawn Grove
Jamaicans' work bears fruit

Jamaican workers congregate in camps in Fawn Grove and Brodbecks.

When wartime labor-strapped fruit growers need pickers, they contract with these British subjects. Councils, with elected officials, govern the two camps working on that summer's bounty. One leader is Elijah Lewis, a teacher in Jamaican schools. The Jamaicans are to return to their homeland by Oct. 1.

"The Jamaican accent baffles county residents, totally unprepared to hear English with a British accent complete with broad a's and extra h's," a newspaper reported. "The rising inflection of their speech, however, gives their speech a Latin emphasis so that it is difficult to understand Jamaicans speaking among themselves."

1950: South Korea
Neglect, racism undid 24th

Lt. Leon Gilbert of York, a decorated World War II combat soldier, refuses an order to lead an assault on a Korean hill.

The action takes place after North Korean forces surprise U.S. forces in invading South Korea to kick off the Korean War. Later, Gilbert said an attack against a bigger force would be suicide for his all-black regiment.

He faces court-martial and is sentenced to death. President Truman commutes the sentence, but Gilbert serves five years in prison. In 1996, an official Army report noted that Gilbert's regiment performed poorly in the early years of the Korean conflict, as did many white units. But the report attributed the failures to neglect, inferior white leadership and institutional racism.

"There was no single reason for what happened (to the 24th)," the report stated. "An aggressive enemy, old and worn equipment, inexperience at all levels, leadership failures high and low, casualties among key personnel and a lack of bonding and cohesion in some units all played their part. There was no lack of courage among the officers and men."

1940s-1950s: York County
Community involvement

Seven-year-old Robert Woodyard, son of Mr. and Mrs. Stephen Woodyard, York, wins the flower box division in a garden contest sponsored by the Pinafore Club of Crispus Attucks Community Center in 1948. The youngest of 12 children, Robert is a second-grade pupil at Aquilla Howard School. Angel wing, wax plants, lilies, snow balls, dahlias and asters are among the flowers he raised in the yard.

The Brotherly Love Elks Lodge's new annex on South Park Avenue near Princess Street provides food, soft drinks and a place to rest for the delegates to the state-wide convention and the spectators in town for the parade in 1947. The annex was completed to house the activities of the Junior Elks and other auxiliaries of the lodge. Grand Exalted Ruler J. Findley Wilson congratulated Dr. George W. Bowles and his committee for their 'excellent' work on the annex.

Hannah Johnson, 14-year-old daughter of Mr. and Mrs. Marshall Johnson, York, poses with some of the zinnias and roses that won her top honors in the Crispus Attucks contest for flower gardens in 1948. The youngest of three children, Hannah is a ninth-grade student at Phineas Davis Junior High School.

Roger L. Tyler, Marilee Jones and children's committee members Mrs. Nesher Chapman and Mrs. Frances Boatwright judge posters drawn by children in a Lodge 3118 contest to publicize a national meeting of the Grand United Order of Odd Fellows in Washington, D.C., in 1956. The judging would be completed in time for an upcoming meeting, which would also include honors for elder lodge members Basil Biggs and Stanley T. Murray, and Bertha Redman, longtime member of the Household of Ruth 699. The lodge also planned to honor the order's founder, Peter Ogden, at another meeting at Faith Presbyterian Church.

1954: York
Desegregation proceeds in York

York City School District officials say they "obviously...shall plan" to meet U.S. Supreme Court directives enforcing the ban on racial segregation in schools.

Such a ban already exists in Pennsylvania, but York has two all-black elementary schools at the time of the U.S. Supreme Court's Brown vs. Board of Education decision. The district assigns black students to the Smallwood and Aquilla Howard schools, which have no set geographical boundaries unlike other city elementary schools. However, black parents can request reassignment to other schools, and those requests are granted, if space is available.

Even before the Supreme Court's decision, black children apparently are enrolling in the city's integrated schools. The number of students in the black schools is down. Supt. Arthur W. Ferguson notes the district has been moving toward desegregation.

In the early 1950s, for example, black children began attending the all-white Princess Street elementary school. Junior high schools and the senior high school had been integrated for some time.

City schools fully integrate in September 1955. Officials said the first days of school went without incident.

Druesilla Jenkins, a black woman teaching at Alexander D. Goode Elementary School, agreed years later that the school year started smoothly.

"I don't think I had any qualms about integration," she said. "It was the law of the land."

Today, some York blacks recall the struggle in adjusting from a school world of black teachers and classmates to one where blacks were in a minority.

In the mid-1950s, the first black student entered another York school — the York Hospital School of Nursing. Senie Hill from Johnstown graduated in 1957.

"She was very nice, and as far as we were concerned, she was simply a member of the family of sister nurses," classmate Rosemary Bentzel recalled.

Bentzel related a time when a waitress at a York restaurant would not serve Hill, there with a group of nurses.

"We girls instantly got up," she said, "and left."

Cartoonist Walt Partymiller comments on segregation of York's elementary schools prior to the Brown vs. Board of Education decision that bans such racial grouping.

This photo appeared in the January 1958 'Spotlight on Schools,' a York City School District publication. It is one of the York County Heritage Trust's earliest photographs of integrated classrooms in York.

The May festival attracted hundreds each year to segregated Smallwood School. Here, sixth-grader Barbara Washington, 11, is crowned queen by first-grader Willie Mae Walker, 6, at the 1952 May festival at Smallwood.

1951: York
Doctor's deeds surpass calling

Dr. George W. Bowles, known for his interracial work, dies at the age of 72.

Bowles practiced medicine in York from 1906, the year he graduated from Howard University School of Medicine, until his death.

He headed the National Medical Association in 1938 and was active in medical organizations at every level. He served on several governmental commissions and appeared before a special U.S. Senate committee on appropriations for syphilis eradication.

But he was best known in the York community, along with the Rev. Thomas Montouth, as a spokesman on issues affecting blacks.

The York High grad chaired the York Inter-Racial Commission for six years and helped found the Crispus Attucks Community Center.

His long obituary story in a local newspaper ends with the following accomplishment: He was the oldest male member of the Small Memorial A.M.E. Zion Church.

James L. Jamison was another pioneering black doctor. Jamison, a member of the county medical society, was a longtime physician in Wrightsville, practicing in the late 19th- and early-20th centuries.

His son, James L. Jamison Jr., became secretary of the New York YMCA after successful stints as a school principal in Pennsylvania, Maryland and New Jersey.

1952: Springettsbury Township
County feels earth, population shift

Earthmoving equipment scrapes sod and dirt from a Springettsbury Township farm to prepare the way for America's foremost manufacturer of earthmoving equipment — Caterpillar.

Cat moves more than York County soil. The company changes the industrial environment, pulling skilled labor from other manufacturers and introducing a higher wage scale to the county marketplace.

But Cat moves itself, too. This towering wage scale will lead to the demise of the facility in the late 1990s.

Within sight of the Cat plant, workers construct tract after tract of homes. The ex-soldiers and their new brides, now back home from the factories, are starting families, and a demand develops for housing in York and elsewhere.

The city hits its highest population of 59,704 in 1950, and the county's population increases by more than 13 percent since 1940. Few building sites are available in the city, so developers create suburbs, showing a voracious appetite for county farmland.

Many vets gain employment at Cat, live in Haines Acres and shop at Sears in the new York County Shopping Center.

The attractions of suburban life started a decline in city population that continues today. In 1960, York's population declined to 54,504. The 2000 U.S. Census placed York's population at 40,862.

Cat brings another element to York County: outside ownership. One by one, locally owned industries sell to companies with out-of-town headquarters.

The crowning point comes in 1988 when out-of-town owner Cadbury USA sells York Peppermint Patties, that favorite chocolate-covered peppermint creme candy, to Hershey Foods Corp. Hershey moves the candymaking operations to Reading in 1989.

The company has no plans, a spokesman said, to rename the cool breeze candy "Reading Peppermint Pattie."

1957: York
Orr builds on opportunities

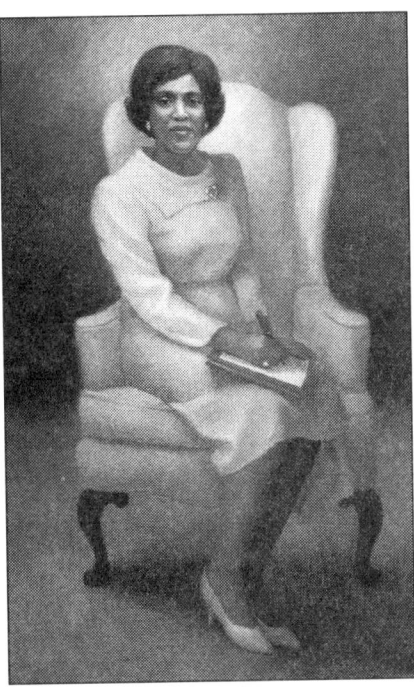

Eula Mae Nimmons Orr

David M. Orr

David M. Orr becomes assistant pastor of Shiloh Baptist Church.

Known for his deep religious faith, Orr is also noted for his business acumen. Orr starts his business life in York in the late 1920s, selling pancake syrup door-to-door in the black community. He later owns a restaurant, barbershop, grocery store and Fisher Refuse Collection Company.

Orr and his wife, the former Eula Mae Nimmons, build the trash collection business into a company that services many residences and commercial interests in the York area.

They sold the company to L.P. Leber III in 1979. Waste Management acquired the company in 1981.

1961: York
Maynard launches distinguished career

Robert C. Maynard relaxes at his desk during his reporting days with The York Gazette and Daily.

Robert C. Maynard begins his daily newspaper career with The York Gazette and Daily, predecessor to the York Daily Record, after unsuccessfully applying to more than 300 newspapers.

He soon begins work on answering the question: What makes people poor in America?

"This place is like every other place, just smaller," a Gazette and Daily editor told Maynard. "Here we can examine in microcosm those things you knew and saw in New York City in macrocosm."

Maynard covers many government boards.

"We sometimes were too busy to examine the distinctions between the microcosm and macrocosm of much of anything," he later wrote.

After several years in York, Maynard moves to The Washington Post and, later, becomes owner of The Oakland Tribune. He died in 1993, one of the most powerful and respected black journalists in America.

Maynard was awarded an honorary degree in 1984 from York College of Pennsylvania.

Maynard receives an honorary degree from York College in 1984. Former York College President Robert Iosue is at right.

The York community recognized other black people in the 1980s and 1990s including: Doctor of humane letters, York College, Bobby Simpson, 1989; Law Day Liberty Bell Award, Simpson, 1986; William Penn High School Hall of Fame, Marie White Bell, Theodore Holmes, Woody Bennett, Reuben Washington, Ernest E. Hartzog, Loretta Claiborne, Maulana Karenga and Chris Doleman.

1956: West York
Nurse joins West Side Hospital staff

White

Mary E. White graduates from Beaumont School of Nursing in Philadelphia and works at Doctors' Hospital before returning home to York.

In York, she cannot find a nursing position at either York or West Side hospitals and takes a position as an elevator operator at The Yorktowne Hotel. She becomes acquainted with Georgia Stum, who persuades her to try a fourth time for employment at West Side, the West York predecessor of Memorial Hospital.

Betty L. Carver, director of nursing, hires her, making White the first black nurse to work there. White works for the hospital until her retirement 23 years later.

A Memorial Hospital history states that she was treated well.

"Patients admired her, according to Mrs. White's colleagues, who also honored her for her dedication and warmth," the history states.

1957: Philadelphia
Green Circle gets worthy beginning

Gladys Rawlins, a black woman born in York, creates Green Circle while working for the Society of Friends Race Relations Committee near Philadelphia.

The program, designed to develop an appreciation of human differences and to encourage self-worth, has since spread to 41 states and is used widely in York County schools.

1959: York
Stroke claims ex-slave in April

Mary Virginia Carter, believed to be 114 years old, dies on the anniversary of Abraham Lincoln's death.

The former slave was believed to be the oldest woman in the state.

The York woman's exact birth date is unknown, but in middle age she met the son of a former master. The two calculated her age to that date, and she kept track after that. Several years before her death, she recalled being sold as a slave three times.

"It was an awful thing," she recalled. "They bought us like animals."

1959: York
Street gains name from Aunt Jo

Johanna Harris, who played an active role in the community, dies.

Her friends and neighbors call her Aunt Jo.

"We absorbed a lot of good things just by working with her and watching her," Frances Ammon, a friend, said after Aunt Jo's death.

To honor her, a lane near her West Princess Street home is named Aunt Jo Lane in 1980.

1960: York County
Chamber 'firsts' honor successes

Anna Ramage becomes the York Chamber of Commerce's first woman director.

She rallies female members to hold a reception for new teachers. In 1997, women operated about 225 chamber-member businesses.

Jake Rhoades Window Cleaning became one of the first minority-owned chamber members in the 1960s. Bobby Simpson of Crispus Attucks Association became the first minority director in 1986.

1960: York
Baptists buy a church home

The First Assembly of God congregation moves from its 23-year-old church on Pershing Avenue, making its building available for Bethlehem Baptist Church.

The Rev. John A. Blackwell leads his congregation in the purchase of the building.

The congregation, organized in 1926 under the Rev. Cornelius Nelson Odom of Bamberg, S.C., burned its mortgage in 1973.

1963: Washington, D.C.

Dr. Martin Luther King Jr. describes his dream that white and black children would someday happily play together, as these York students listen near the Lincoln Memorial in the March for Freedom in August 1963.

County's busloads March for Freedom

Ten busloads of black and white York County residents travel to Washington, D.C., in August 1963 to observe the March for Freedom, known today as the March on Washington.

The 350 county residents join about 100,000 other people from across the country in the demonstration for civil rights. Last-minute registrations swell the number attending from York, William D. Barber, local event organizer, said. About 100 of the county group march from the Washington Monument to the Lincoln Memorial.

March organizers hand out pledge cards. "It was an affirmation of their commitment to the struggle for jobs and freedom," a newspaper reported, "and a pledge that they will not relax until the victory is won."

The highlight for most is the Rev. Martin Luther King Jr.'s "I Have a Dream" speech.

Donnie Breland, a postal clerk, watches the speech on television. "I was thinking Martin Luther King had a connection to God — like Moses," Breland said years later. "Being African-American, I have to say he was like a black Moses."

Several other gatherings marked the summer and fall of 1963.

A service honoring four young black girls killed in the Sept. 15 bombing of a Birmingham, Ala., church attracts a mixed audience of blacks and whites, numbering in the hundreds, to Penn Park. The Rev. George Spells, former York pastor, speaks at the service sponsored by the Peaceful Committee for Immediate Action in York.

The Rev. Spells condemns Alabama Gov. George Wallace for his disinterest in preventing the deaths. The indignation of America's founders against British tyranny, he said, is the same now felt by blacks.

York County residents step forward to aid the victims' families. The Peaceful Committee for Immediate Action mailed a check of more than $800 to the Birmingham Children's Memorial Fund.

Maurice Peters, Ettie Lambert, Beverly Beatty, Ivan A. Reeves, Carlton D. Trotman and Halmon L. Banks III are among the leaders of the Peaceful Committee.

In another protest against racial discrimination in York, the Rev. Thomas Montouth and the Rev. Richard Manning are among speakers addressing 1,500 people gathered at Penn Park.

1962: Atlanta, Ga.
Lawson, King Jr. work together

The Rev. Leslie Lawson, later pastor of Small Memorial A.M.E. Zion Church, flies to Atlanta to join Dr. Martin Luther King Jr. and other ministers in planning strategy for the civil rights movement.

Lawson and King have been acquainted since meeting at a march in Bridgeport, Conn., where Lawson was a minister and teacher.

After they complete their business in Atlanta, they pray on the courthouse steps. Others join them, but police come with a different purpose. King, Lawson and the other ministers land in jail for causing a public nuisance.

The group spends five days in jail but is never brought to trial. On the day he is to be released from the Atlanta jail, Lawson refuses to leave and demands a trial to show the group's innocence. King shakes his head.

"Don't be a fool," King tells Lawson. "If they're letting you out, go."

Lawson, living in York, remembered King on the 30th anniversary of his slaying: "There was a man that really, really could forbear. He was a strong man."

1962: York
Howard School knocked down

York City School District sells Aquilla Howard School, a former school for black children on East King Street, for $11,000.

The four-classroom elementary school was later demolished to make way for an apartment complex parking lot.

York's other black school, the eight-classroom Smallwood School on Pershing Avenue, becomes a language arts building on William Penn High School's campus in 1958 and is razed several years later to allow for high school expansion.

1963: York
York's civil rights education 'limited'

Hal Brown, former William Penn High School and San Diego State University basketball star, returns to York to visit family and becomes temporarily involved in civil rights work.

He marches as part of a demonstration in York.

Brown, a teacher in San Diego, is chairman of that city's chapter of Congress of Racial Equality, which he helped to organize.

"I see York now as a place which offers limited opportunities to the Negro," he told a York newspaper, "and as a community where education in the field of civil rights among whites and Negroes is very limited."

1964: Dallastown
Neighbors welcome couple from Bucks

William and Daisy Myers, who had met resistance as the first blacks to live in the planned community of Levittown, Bucks County, in 1957, move with their children to York County.

Their new neighbors bring them cake, candies and best wishes when they settle into an all-white neighborhood.

"No comparison," like chocolate and cheese, Daisy Myers said in 1997.

Daisy Myers later becomes principal of Arthur W. Ferguson Elementary School in York and a secretary in a federal government office in York.

In Levittown, the reception had been different. Mobs gathered outside their house, burned crosses and unfurled a Confederate flag. More than 500 people gathered outside their home one week after they moved in. State troopers pushed the crowd back, at one point charging with batons swinging.

Mob activity subsided after that. Pennsylvania's governor called out the state police to protect the Myers family. George Leader, a York County native, was that governor.

1966: West York
York native named aide to Farrakhan

Maurice Peters Jr. remembers the day in 1959 that his family moved to a suburban neighborhood, the only black family in Shiloh.

Neighbors blocked the movers' way to the new house.

"If something happens to my children, then something might happen to your children," Peters' father told him.

The memory is seared into Peters' memory. "Every October 28, I don't fail to remember," he said.

Peters graduates with distinction from West York Area High School in 1966. He later graduates from Case Western Reserve University School of Medicine and faces a bright career as a surgeon. In 1980, he meets Louis Farrakhan, a leader of the Nation of Islam. Farrakhan gives Peters his present name, Abdul Alim Muhammad.

Peters

In 1988, Dr. Muhammad becomes the national spokesman for Farrakhan, who is known for his anti-white and anti-Semitic remarks.

"Minister Farrakhan is the most decent person I've ever met in my life," the county native said. "People have misquoted him or distorted his views or outright lied."

The county has another connection to Farrakhan. Arthur Magida, former York Gazette and Daily reporter and later senior editor at the Baltimore Jewish Times, wrote "Prophet of Rage: A Life of Louis Farrakhan and His Nation."

The book, published in 1998, is the first biography of the black leader.

1966: Los Angeles
York native creates Kwanzaa

Maulana Karenga, a York native, founds the African-American celebration of Kwanzaa in 1966.

Karenga, then known as Ron Everett, graduated from William Penn High School in 1958 and went on to receive doctorates from United States International University and the University of Southern California. He became interested in black studies and issues facing black Americans.

The seven-day Kwanzaa celebration starts on Dec. 26. The observance marks black cultural unity.

1967: York
Graduates gather at fairgrounds

The William Penn High School senior class scores two firsts: It elects the school's first black homecoming queen and holds its graduation ceremony at the York Fairgrounds.

Linda Woodward receives the homecoming crown.

A graduating class of about 600 students dictates a move to the fairgrounds.

An increasing diversity, however, does not mean the high school escapes the impact of racial tension and violence that riddles York in the late 1960s. School officials shut down William Penn for four days in April 1970 after three students are injured in stabbing incidents. The school reopens without incident as 40 percent of the students stay home.

Teams of parents, working in black-white pairs, and Community Progress Council workers patrol the hallways.

1967: York
Quality schools Chapman's goal

Mortician W. Russell Chapman becomes the first black person to serve on the York City School Board, appointed to fill the vacancy of H. DeForest Hardinge.

Running as a Democrat two years later, he wins the highest number of votes for an elected school seat. Chapman becomes known as an independent thinker.

"You could classify him as a liberal or as a conservative," board President Ralph F. Runkle said. "He would weigh every issue, try to think of what would happen eventually if he voted a certain way, then make up his mind — and that was it."

He is known for seeking quality education for all students. "When he said . . . that he is concerned not with black or white or green men — just the man — I believe he meant it," board member Edith A. Barber said.

In ill health, he casts swing votes that back a school busing plan to gain racial balance in school and designate Martin Luther King Jr.'s birthday a holiday in the city schools.

Four days before his death in 1971, the board meets in the Chapman home on the busing plan. From a chair at the top of the steps, he states, "I'm voting for it."

He died on Martin Luther King Jr.'s birthday.

Mildred Chapman, his wife, was a leader in the community, too. She directed the Crispus Attucks Community Center Women and Girls Program.

Other pioneering black school board members in York County include: Doris A. Sweeney, the first black woman elected to the city school board in 1977, serving until 1987; and Daniel A. Elby, whose two terms as the only black member of the Central York School Board ended in 2001.

Today, eight of the nine York City School Board members, including board President Jeffrey Kirkland, are black.

1968: York
Speakers honor King's legacy

About 500 people, standing in a drizzle at York's Penn Park, hear black leaders speak against violence four days after the death of the Rev. Dr. Martin Luther King Jr. 'I have a nightmare,' said the Rev. John A. Blackwell, in drawing from the assassinated civil rights leader's most famous speech. 'Could we find men here today who really believe in non-violence?' Blackwell asked the audience. 'This is my nightmare, as I read the newspapers today, that men across the nation have totally misunderstood Martin Luther King's purpose in living and his purpose in dying.'

Kirkland

c. 1968: Lower Chanceford Twp.
Services end at Batty's Chapel

Paul Cevis is the last pastor to serve Mt. Olive A.M.E. Zion Church, sometimes called Batty's Chapel, as the church closes its doors in the late 1960s.

For many years, the Lower Chanceford Township church is home to the Batty, Murray, Barton and Patterson families who worshipped there.

Today, the church stands in poor condition.

1968-69: York
Riots reveal long-standing racial attitudes

As race becomes a political and social flashpoint in the United States, riots over two summers paralyze York, causing two deaths and more than 40 injuries.

Officer Henry C. Schaad, a 22-year-old York patrolman, is shot July 18, 1969, after bullets pierce an armored police vehicle in which he was riding. He suffers five wounds and dies on Aug. 1.

Three days after the Schaad shooting, Lillie Belle Allen, a 27-year-old black woman visiting from Aiken, S.C., is shot to death while on her way to a Manchester Township supermarket.

National Guardsmen arrive in York with armored vehicles to help restore order.

The riots culminate years of what appeared to be racially motivated incidents, practices and attitudes in the county.

For example, U.S. Congressman Adam J. Glossbrenner from York County presented a petition in 1867 to the House giving white immigrants suffrage and other rights afforded the recently freed slaves.

A York newspaper suggested if the petition had covered blacks, it would have gained speedy acceptance: "Had it been an application from negroes for an appropriation of money out of the public treasury, or a petition for the passage of an act recognizing the superiority of the African over the White race, it would have been promptly acted on."

In 1904, a newspaper reported that more than 700 members of "Monumental City Doctors' Coachmen association of negroes yesterday descended in a dark cloud on York." Four officers were assigned to keep the visitors from Baltimore "within the bounds of decency inside the city limits."

"Vulgar and repulsive as are the actions of most of these excursionists, yesterday's consignment was no exception," the newspaper reported.

In 1940, a York police officer shot a black youth in the leg as he was running away from other officers after committing a minor offense.

"It is a good thing the youth was of no consequence in the community, otherwise there might be visited on the person who shot him severe punishment for his senseless and unnecessary use of a death dealing weapon," a newspaper editorial said.

An academic who studied York in the 1960s summarized the racial picture: "These small incidents of bias that blacks as individuals endured daily added up over time to a tangible blot on the community. The most evident result of an endemic prejudice that systematically denied blacks good jobs, that refused to offer blacks social standing and that excluded blacks from the community's power structure was the rotten accumulation of slums at York's core."

The impact of the riots remains evident today. The once-bustling downtown became a place that many county residents started to avoid.

Thirty-two years after the riots ended, prosecutors charged nine white men, including then-Mayor Charlie Robertson, in the murder of Allen and two black men in the death of Schaad.

The legal proceedings attracted more national and international media attention than any other county court case since the Hex Murder trials of the late 1920s.

Armored carriers are a common sight on the streets of York during the 1969 race riots. For one summer week, York's mayor imposes curfews, and the Pennsylvania State Police and state National Guard provide assistance.

1970: York
Charrette's therapy defuses conflict

Hundreds of York residents attend a charrette, in which all parts of the community come together to pour out complaints and call for specific reforms.

The charrette is called a kind of civic group therapy. The multi-day event addresses social and economic problems that had led to racial strife the previous two summers. It is credited with defusing tension through meaningful discussion among various segments of the community.

Many attending the charrette indicate that a canine unit, used by police since 1962, represents a major threat to civic harmony.

Almost since their introduction, the police dogs had been controversial. Many in the black community believed the dogs were used indiscriminately against them.

Responding to such criticism in 1963, York Mayor John L. Snyder defended their use, calling them "one of the greatest assets to the police department." They helped police track down violators and "are also a support to a policeman when necessary to cope with a group," he wrote.

Three years after the charrette ended, York's public safety officials said the city's K-9 Corps of police dogs would disband.

The charrette takes place in the early stages of a new administration in York City Hall.

Eli Eichelberger had replaced Jessie M. Gross, who took over the position temporarily after the death of Snyder in late 1969.

Snyder, a three-term mayor, had drawn blame for contributing to or not trying to combat the effects of turbulent times in York — racial tension, decline of city population and flight to suburbia.

"Snyder's mayorship, especially in the 1960s, will be remembered for its confrontation with change," a historian wrote.

Still, The York Gazette and Daily, Snyder's longtime nemesis, commented on Snyder's death, "But even the most vocal of Mr. Snyder's critics felt that he was a man of honesty and integrity, whose personal character was above reproach."

1972: York
Crispus Attucks gains stability

Officials break ground for a new Crispus Attucks Community Center on South Duke Street.

"Many neighborhoods throughout the country have used the services of their community center to improve the quality of life in their community," a membership report stated. The center goes through a half dozen directors during the next seven years before Bobby Simpson, an employee at Caterpillar, takes over in 1979.

Simpson has since headed the agency as it has become a center for recreation, day care, housing rehabilitation, economic development, job placement and a convener of community meetings.

Simpson

Today, Crispus Attucks also operates a charter school and is in the third phase of a project to improve the Boundary Avenue area.

On the 50th anniversary of the first black to play Major League Baseball in 1997, York NAACP President M. Baba Whisler counted Simpson as one of York's Jackie Robinsons.

1974: York
Borom takes seat on city council

About a dozen people attend the swearing in of Roy O. Borom to a position on York City Council. Borom, believed to be the first black to serve on council, replaces Allan M. Dameshek, who resigned.

City council members Elizabeth N. Marshall and James R. Vogelsong watch as Judge Albert G. Blakey III administers the oath. A year later, voters elect Borom to a four-year term.

Borom had come to York County to head the Crispus Attucks Community Center six years before. "The current role of the Crispus Attucks executive director should encompass a commitment to engage the larger community in a mutual identification and alteration of those external forces ... ," Borom said upon taking over his duties in York County, "that represent barriers to the equal opportunity and full citizenship status for Negroes and other underprivileged community residents."

Wm. Lee Smallwood was York's second black city councilman, serving from the late 1970s until today, with a short break in service in the early 1980s.

Ray Crenshaw was also a council member through the 1990s, gaining appointment in 1992 and leading the ticket for election in 1993.

Smallwood

Crenshaw

1974: York
City organizes civil rights agency

York City Council adopts ordinances creating a city Human Relations Commission.

The agency works to promote civil rights and increase tolerance. Halmon L. Banks III chairs the commission, and Carlton D. Trotman serves as the first director.

Ten years later, the agency moves into an East Princess Street building that had served as controversial Mayor John L. Snyder's home and insurance office. The building serves as the commission's office today.

1975: York
County selects Chapman for office

County voters elect Mattie Chapman, an Albany, Ga., native, to the post of county prothonotary in 1975.

She is thought to be the first black woman elected to county office. She had started in the prothonotary's office as a clerk 19 years earlier.

The Democrat leads the ticket in winning a second term. Republicans support the incumbent and so do local attorneys.

"They (attorneys) knew how well she ran the office," longtime attorney Nevin Stetler said. "She hired all good people, and they did their job."

1975: York
Learning center garners praise

On its first anniversary, the Crispus Attucks Early Learning Center receives high marks from the state Department of Welfare office of day care services.

The highest praise comes for the teachers who are "constantly involved" and "neither remote or lackadaisical in their program participation."

Dolores Borom directs the program, which operates under an advisory board headed by Timothy Warfield.

The learning center plans to expand its day care services to include 30 half-day children and 100 children in grades 1-5.

1977: York
Bible Tabernacle opens doors

Bible Tabernacle organizes as a congregation.

Two years later, the congregation moves into a former bowling alley at 361 S. Pine St., a building it occupies today.

Carl Scott left his position managing the data processing department at AMF Inc., now Harley-Davidson, to found the church.

"I cried that day," Diane Scott, the pastor's wife, later said. "I was afraid we were going to lose the house."

"They didn't," a newspaper reported. "They gained a church."

1980: York
Different faiths take root in county

York's community is becoming more diverse, as reflected in the names of several houses of worship forming in the 1980s and 1990s.

The Cristo Salvador Spanish Catholic Church locates in a building on East South Street; First Spanish United Methodist Church on South Queen Street; and Noor Mosque on South George Street.

The mosque opens in 1985 in the former Catholic Social Services building. About 60 area Muslims, most members of the Ahmadiyya sect, previously met in homes.

Today, about 25 central Pennsylvania families, or about 125 people, gather at Noor Mosque for weekly prayer. The gathering includes many white and black Americans.

The Black Muslims and other Muslim movements also have adherents in York County.

1982: Plainfield, N.J.
Holliday heads to Cleveland

Supt. Frederick D. Holliday of the Plainfield, N.J., school system leaves to head Cleveland schools.

He led York City schools from 1974-81, the district's first black superintendent.

"Dr. Holliday tried to make sure that every child in the district had the opportunity to learn at their own level," Doris Sweeney, former school director, said.

Holliday is credited with instituting programs through private industry to help lower the dropout rate and establishing an alternative school that gave problem students a chance to graduate.

York City Council member Wm. Lee Smallwood believes Holliday transformed the school system.

"He turned around not only the image of York schools but the educational attainments as well," he said.

The city Civil Rights Commission holds an annual awards luncheon to commemorate Holliday's life's work.

1979: York
Black officer leads city force

Thomas Chatman, left, succeeds Wayne Ruppert, right, as York's police chief in 1979. Chatman is the first black man to hold the position. Chatman started with the York Police Department in 1956, one of its first black officers. Wilbur Spells had been the first in 1955. Chatman rose through the ranks. After his stint as chief, he headed the city's parking bureau, retiring in 1997. Since Chatman's term, two other black officers have served in top city police positions. Russell Clanagan served as police commissioner in the 1990s, and Michael Hill serves as chief of police today.

Holliday

Warfield

1983: York
Warfield's sax launches career

Tenor saxophonist Tim Warfield, a 1983 William Penn High School grad, tours with jazz legends in the 1990s and records a CD, "A Cool Blue," on a major label.

He is one of several black county residents who gain national reputations in the music field.

Rock and Roll Hall of Famer Charlie Thomas of the Drifters, who had performed such hits as "Under the Boardwalk" and "There Goes My Baby," lives in York today.

The late Moses Rascoe, a York resident, had played his blues guitar at major U.S. folk festivals and was particularly popular in Europe.

1984: York
'Roots' author part of celebration

Alex Haley speaks in York on themes from his best-selling "The Autobiography of Malcolm X" (1965) and "Roots" (1976).

"What it's ('Roots') has given me," Haley told a newspaper, "is a much broader perspective of we human beings...And the biggest single problem on this earth for all of us ...is our desperate need to know more about each other."

Also as part of the Black History Month observance, Billy Baker, a black artist, displays his work at Martin Library, and an exhibition opens displaying Dolores Borom's black doll collection.

1985: Wrightsville
Many veterans buried in cemetery

Alverta S. "Bertie" Bear is the only member of the Mount Pisgah Cemetery Association living in Wrightsville.

So she takes care of what she calls the "colored cemetery," the burial place of longtime Wrightsville residents with the names of Fairfax, Forman, Barton, Green, Jones, Johnson, Little, Swailes, Cowan, Moore, Woodyard and Williams, among many others.

The cemetery is the resting place of black veterans from the Civil War through the Korean War.

William Henry Bear, Alverta Bear's husband and a World War I veteran, is buried there.

And Bertie Bear's age?

"Can you keep a secret?" she asks a reporter. "So can I."

1986: Asheboro, N.C.
Physician makes York house call

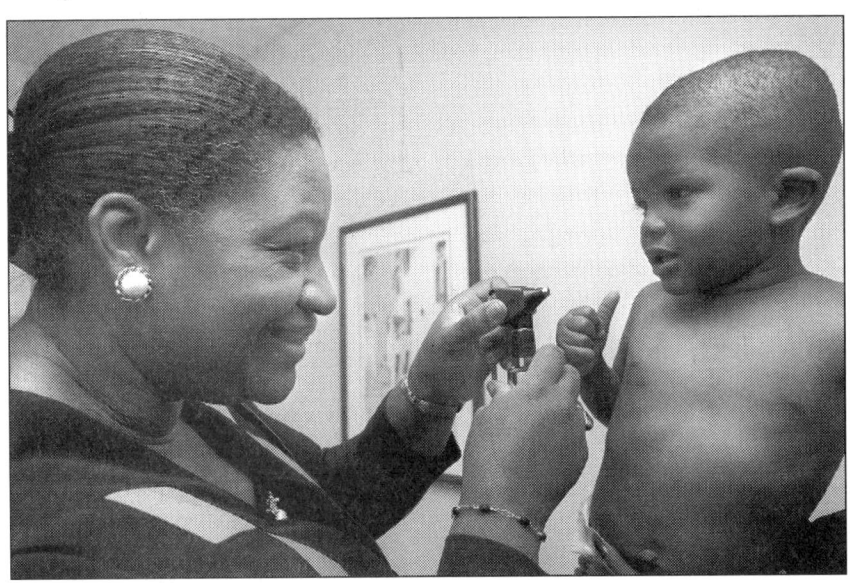

Dr. Deborah McMillan examines NaGus Griggs during a routine checkup at Yorktowne Family Medicine on Bannister Street. Years earlier in 1986, McMillan answered a York reporter's questions between seeing patients in Asheboro, N.C. Yes, she replied, she might like to practice medicine in her hometown of York someday. Two weeks later, Yorktowne Family Medical Associates contacted her. 'Around this same time, I had a calling from the Lord to go back to York,' she stated years later. 'I thought if I were supposed to go that He'd provide a place for me.' Soon, the 1968 graduate of William Penn High School is treating patients in York and remains in practice today.

1986: Washington, D.C.
William Penn grad moves to Library

Debra Newman Ham, a graduate of William Penn High School in 1966, becomes a black history specialist in the manuscript division of the Library of Congress.

The historian cares for papers belonging to Booker T. Washington, Frederick Douglass and Thurgood Marshall.

In 1995, she moves to Morgan State University, where she teaches history and is chief curator of a major Library of Congress exhibit, "The African American Odyssey." The exhibit documented black America's quest for full citizenship.

1988: York
Shiloh Baptist burns mortgage

Six years after purchasing its Pershing Avenue building from Christ United Methodist Church, Shiloh Baptist Church holds a mortgage-burning ceremony.

The church, founded in 1883, bought the building at a cost of $110,000 and paid off its 20-year, $82,500 mortgage in six years. The Rev. Richard Manning was pastor of the growing congregation when the new house of worship was purchased.

1989: Harrisburg
Star football player dies

William Penn High School football player Lewis Atwater dies a month after lapsing into a coma.

He suffers a cerebral hemorrhage in the Bearcat season opener against Central Dauphin East.

"I've had hundreds and hundreds of kids who have played for me," Jeff Ruby, Atwater's

Atwater

coach, said. "I'm not just saying this because he passed away. Before practice this year, I told Lewie's father, 'Your kid is the greatest all-around kid I've had the privilege to be around.'"

York's Human Relations Commission later established the Lewis Atwater III Memorial Award to recognize students who excel academically and in community service.

Chaz Amos Green, Jazmin Byers, Oziel Bones, Kerry Kirkland Jr., Parag Patel, Glaed Rojas and Sandie Walker are among those receiving the award.

1989: York
NBC features adoptive mom

Barbara Tremitiere retires from Tressler Lutheran Service Associates as a nationally recognized figure in the field of adoption.

She gains expertise at home. The mother of 15 gave birth to three children, and she and her husband, Bill, adopted 12 others of various ethnic backgrounds.

In 1987, four of the Tremitieres' adopted children graduated from William Penn High School — Mark, Monique, Nicolle and Chantel. This caught the eye of NBC-TV news.

"We found out that Barbara Tremitiere is recognized as an authority on transracial adoption," NBC correspondent Bill Schechner said, "but the thing that strikes me about her is that she practices what she preaches. She translates what she says and puts it in her own life."

1989: York
Visit spurs talk of history center

The planned visit to York by professor Helen Johnson, a York native, sparks discussion in the black community about a black history and cultural center.

Johnson, who runs the Armstead-Johnson Foundation for Theater Research in New York, collects thousands of costumes, photographs and scripts.

Jean M. Downs, a retired elementary school teacher and collector of black history memorabilia, said finding items for a museum would be no problem. She told a newspaper that she has enough items herself to fill a building.

1993: Coulsontown
For residents, town is paradise

Marian Green lived in Coulsontown all her life.

"It's peaceful here," she said in 1993, "and peacefulness is one of the pleasures of Coulsontown."

The focal point of this village, set just 500 yards north of the Mason-Dixon Line near Delta, is four stone quarrymen's cottages, dating back to the 1840s. The Welsh quarrymen worked the area's slate quarries. The town's population peaked at about 75 decades ago.

Twenty people reside in the town in 1993, 19 of them are black.

"We don't worry about the things people worry about in the city," Green said. "You know, drugs and crime. It's still safe and friendly here. Most of us go to church together at Trinity A.M.E. Zion Church."

Bernard Hawkins converted an old Coulsontown quarryman's shed into an outbuilding in which to store tools.

Marian and Robert Green have lived in Coulsontown for decades.

The sidewalks, steps, shingles and gatepost at this Coulsontown cottage are made of slate from nearby quarries. Even an outhouse, used into the 1990s, has a slate roof.

1991: Hanover
Disturbances rattle town

For two nights in July, racially motivated disturbances — also called "riots," "fracases," and "uprisings" in the media — hit Hanover.

Motorcyclists challenge a racially mixed group of young people on Hanover's Center Square on a hot Saturday evening in July. The confrontation attracts between 200 and 300 onlookers.

The young people exchange racial slurs and obscenities with the bikers and some of the crowd. Hanover police and 27 other municipal police departments respond and defuse the confrontation by 1 a.m.

The next day, Hanover's mayor responds to a gathering of about 500 people confronting a group of youths perched on a West Chestnut Street roof by declaring a state of emergency at 11 p.m. Pennsylvania State Police assist, and curfew enforcement helps police disperse the crowd by midnight.

Police make 51 arrests in the disturbances. A state police investigation alleged that Hanover police did not demonstrate appropriate leadership or have sufficient training to handle civil disobedience. The probe concluded the disturbances stemmed from racist or discriminatory attitudes from some Hanover-area residents.

Hanover United forms to reaffirm positive attitudes toward equality, nondiscrimination and cultural diversity within the community.

1991: York Haven
Supremacist warns of marches

The Hanover disturbances attract white supremacist groups, which organize a march of about 60 members in that borough in November.

Two months later, Albert P. Lentz of York Haven, leader of the county's White United Party, warns 10 municipalities of similar marches.

Lentz dies of a heart attack in 1992, and his body is found two weeks later.

In a 1985 interview, Lentz said he believed the Ku Klux Klan and Adolf Hitler were misunderstood and that Hitler was a great man.

Rick L. Fogel of Red Lion, the Grand Dragon or head of the KKK in Pennsylvania, said the white supremacy movement would continue without Lentz.

1992: York
Local NAACP reorganizes

The York Chapter of the NAACP reorganizes after years of inactivity and takes on voter registration as an initial means of confronting problems facing York's minority community.

"If we unify and mobilize, we have voting power," Randy Christie, the chapter's interim vice president, said.

The revitalized group, headed by 85-year-old Wade Bowers as interim president, sponsors a conference titled "Political action for modern issues."

Cooper

Speakers include: Daisy Myers on the search for common ground; Joseph Douglas, education; Lance Jamison, affordable housing; Ray Crenshaw, voter registration; Michael Jefferson, job training and employment; and Jackie Baker, AIDS research and funding.

In early 1994, the group plays host to a conference of the state NAACP.

Today, Leo Cooper heads the York branch.

1992: York
Group organizes city youth league

Young people in York County participate in the newly formed York City Youth League.

Mark Rhodes, Doug Woodard, Terry Einsig, Edwin Alicea and City Councilman Abe Amoros are members of a group that develops the baseball schedule, accumulates donated equipment and recruits coaches.

Rhodes, a Harley-Davidson employee, spearheads the effort.

"Depending on how you look at it," a newspaper said, "Mark is the father of five, his own son and four daughters, or he is the father of hundreds through the league."

1993: York
Focus on training prompts expansion

Crispus Attucks Community Center dedicates a new $2.5 million educational wing, designed to train leaders of tomorrow.

Those recognized include: John Sexton, 80, the oldest living Crispus Attucks supporter; the late Lance Jamison, property manager of the center's housing program; and Joe Jenkins, scoutmaster at the center for 50 years.

1993: New York
Disabled athlete wins Ashe award

Loretta Claiborne of York receives ESPY's national Arthur Ashe Award for Courage, honoring her determination and lifetime accomplishments in sports.

The previous three winners of the nationally televised Ashe Award were basketball coach Jim Valvano, commentator Howard Cosell and umpire Steve Palermo.

Claiborne, classified soon after birth as being mentally retarded, is a Special Olympics gold medal winner and a Boston Marathoner, among other honors.

"Meet Loretta Claiborne," a York County Association for Retarded Citizens publication said in 1986, "fourth degree black belt karate expert; nationally known marathon runner; sought-after public speaker on dealing with disabilities (who composes her speeches in her head and uses no notes); consistent blue ribbon winner for her knitted clothing at the York Fair; pen pal of Eunice Shriver; caring, articulate and involved."

Claiborne

"She looks for hills," Michael Bortner, a York County state legislator, said in 1986, "just so she can climb them."

1995: Washington, D.C.
Million Man March motivates blacks

About 100 men from York attend the Million Man March in Washington, D.C. Many return inspired.

"We have to love our neighbors as we love ourselves," Michael Walker said. "But if we don't love ourselves, we cannot love our neighbors, and everyone is affected."

The agenda for the future includes starting voter registration drives, networking the black community of York with those in Lancaster and Harrisburg, beginning mentoring programs, and reinvigorating interest in and attracting young people to religious organizations.

"We need to bring the spirituality base back," Walker said. "Spirituality is based on hope."

1996: York
Rusk Report frames poverty's paradoxes

David Rusk, nationally known urban planner, issues "Renewing Our Community: The Rusk Report on the Future of Greater York," creating a wide-ranging debate on the future of the county.

The report suggests several paradoxes:

In the 1990 census, metro York had the nation's fourth-lowest regional poverty rate, but York City scored low with the eighth-worst relative concentration of poverty in America.

Metro York had four times as many poor whites as poor blacks and Latinos combined. More than 80 percent of poor whites lived scattered throughout middle-class areas while almost 80 percent of poor minorities were isolated in York City's impoverished neighborhoods.

York County residents had a strong commitment to small-scale government, but the county's 72 independent municipal and township governments and 16 school systems fostered uncontrolled sprawl, fiscal disparities and greater racial and economic segregation.

1996: York
Emmanuel congregation gains new home

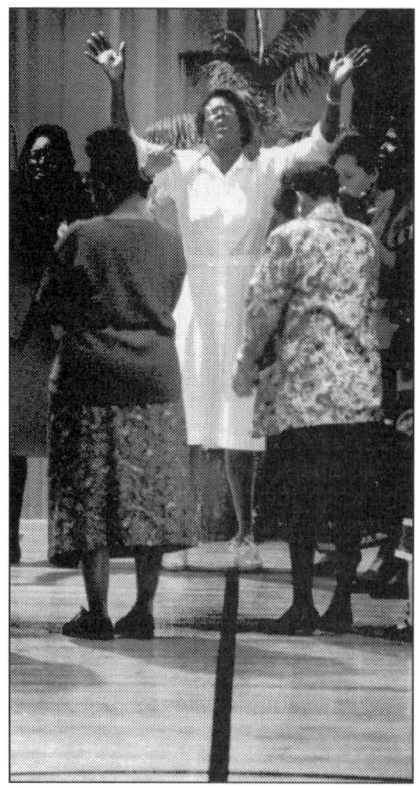

Jural Wye, center, participates in the Emmanuel Church of God in Christ's service in 1996. The congregation met at Crispus Attucks Community Center after its church roof collapsed under the weight of snow.

A handful of Emmanuel Church of God in Christ members are inside their 665 E. Princess St. building when the walls start creaking.

Wind from a winter storm beats against the York building.

The group decides it should leave. Minutes later, half of the roof falls. Broken timber pokes from the heavy snow that has caused the collapse.

The congregation receives more bad news just weeks later. Thieves break into the ruins and help themselves to food for the needy collected there. They also take pots and pans.

"Well, not all of them," Geniece Carroll, who runs the food bank, said. "They left the dinky ones."

About 15 months later, the congregation worships in the former St. Joseph Catholic Church building, just down the road from its destroyed home of more than 50 years.

1997: York
Directory lists minority businesses

A business directory lists more than 200 businesses in York with minority or female ownership.

The directory, compiled by Penn State graduate student Lara Shanabrough, includes a range of black-owned businesses including Washington & Dowling, contractors; The New Hub, clothing; C.N. Patterson, Jr., attorney; and Bouldin Mortuary Inc., funeral services.

No such directory previously existed.

Ben Washington of Washington & Dowling.

1997: York
Well-known window washer passes away

Raymond Rhoades, longtime owner of a window-cleaning service that bore his name, dies at the age of 89.

Rhoades had worked for York Window Cleaning, owned by his father, Charles, and started his own service after World War II.

Meanwhile, his brother, Leroy, continued their father's business. Their work made the Rhoades name synonymous with window cleaning.

Raymond Rhoades even washed windows at home.

"He did the outside," Delores Rhoades told a newspaper, "and I did the inside."

1997: York
TV show focuses on 'Worlds Apart'

Bryan Wade produces "Worlds Apart," a call-in talk show on York Community Access Television about race issues.

Less than a year later, he expands his show's reach to more than a million viewers by broadcasting on WGCB television, picked up by about 40 cable systems. His topics range from ethnicity and its relationship to race, the psychology of racism, genetics and race and hate crimes.

"I don't think I alone can break down any barriers," he told a newspaper, "I just want to give people the information they need to break them down."

A sampling of other blacks who have been involved in the media:

Robert Booker, president of the Community Empowerment Organization, played host to "County Almanac" in 1993. The York-based television show, covering predominantly race-related topics, aired on WSPC-TV (York Cable 4). The first show, which aired in June, focused on public housing.

Ahmad Seifullah, formerly known as Clair Sexton, is a regular letter and guest columnist for York's newspapers.

Ron Martin, a York native, is an anchor for WGAL- TV (Channel 8).

The bylines of Irvin Kittrell III, Russ Crenshaw, Michele Canty, Jeffrey Martin, Eyana McMillan and Leslie Gray Streeter have appeared in local newspapers.

John Dalton published the Heritage News, a monthly newspaper covering the minority community.

1997: Philadelphia
Local women attend march

A group of York County women attend the Million Woman March in Philadelphia, geared to revitalize black families and communities.

Winnie Mandela, former wife of South African President Nelson Mandela, and Maxine Waters, a California congresswoman, are among those speaking.

"It was beautiful," Rosalyn Woodyard told a newspaper. "It was inspirational because the speakers… were saying how we need to bring our communities back to where they used to be when they were so tightly knit."

1996: York
Blacks, whites march

Brad Christine and Robert 'Bunny' Cox play the drums in leading a procession from Living Word Community Church to Mount Moriah Baptist Church's new Prospect Street home. The predominantly white Living Word congregation helped Mount Moriah raise money for the purchase of its new building.

Seven is the order of the day for a mixed crowd of 400 marching between the predominantly white Living Word Community Church and the black Mount Moriah Baptist Church.

Before the march, the Rev. Nathaniel Johnson, pastor of the seven-year-old Mount Moriah congregation, said he would pray for seven minutes, proceed out the door at 7 p.m. and march seven blocks. The number 7 means completeness in the Bible, and the Moriah congregation had just completed settlement on its new Prospect Street building five days before.

"Praise God," the Rev. Johnson proclaimed, "with the help of the Living Word Church and friends of other churches from far and wide, we've done it."

The church successfully meets the challenge of raising $70,000 in 70 days.

1998: York
Neighborhood mom meets goal

Sixty-seven-year-old Margaret Breeland dies at her South Penn Street house.

"Margaret Breeland was foster mother to more than 100 children," a newspaper said, "and a friend to nearly everyone else."

Her name was Margaret, but most people called this neighborhood mom "Mommy."

Shortly before her death, she had suffered a heart attack. Her goal after that was to see her daughter, Yvonne's wedding. She passed this milepost, walking down the aisle without the need of an oxygen tank.

"I feel better now," she told her new son-in-law, Travis Terry, indicating that she could die in peace, "I know you'll take care of my baby."

1999: York County
250th celebration

The York County 250th Anniversary High School Honors Choir performs at the York Expo Center after the conclusion of a 4½-hour parade marking the 250th anniversary of York County in August 1999.

Jeff Washington plays in the brass section for the William Penn High School Marching Band during festivities marking the county's 250th anniversary.

1998: York
Churches move into new buildings

Fairview Full Gospel Missionary Baptist Church worships in a 465 S. Pine St. building that for years was the home of the York Gospel Center.

The Miracle Tabernacle Revival Center previously occupied the building.

The Rev. Robert J. Jamison and "co-pastor" Rebecca Jamison head the Fairview church, which previously worshipped in the former Messiah Lutheran Church building on Prospect Street.

The Cathedral of Praise and Worship purchased the former Messiah church building.

1998: Baltimore
Winning educator hails from York

Stephanie Terry, a first-grade teacher at Ashburton Elementary School, Baltimore, earns a $25,000 national award.

The honors from the Milken Family Foundation recognize the York native's work in raising reading scores and her emphasis on science in reading and writing class work. Four Maryland teachers and 152 instructors in America earn the award.

Terry, a 28-year teacher in urban schools, is one of many achievers who grew up in the close-knit black neighborhood of the 300 block of West Princess Street.

Julia Hines-Harris, former assistant superintendent, York City School District; Dorothy King, assistant professor, Penn State Harrisburg; Marie White Bell, superior court judge, Mount Holly, N.J.; Virginia Hunter, longtime first-grade teacher, York City schools; and Ernest E. Hartzog, school superintendent, Portland, Ore., also grew up in the neighborhood.

1999: York
Former NFL star praises parents

Lenny Moore, Pro Football Hall of Fame running back for the Baltimore Colts, tells the Quarterback Club of York that his parents provided a firm foundation from which he was able to grow.

Moore graduated from high school in Reading and earned football honors at Penn State before his success in the pros.

Lenny Moore's mother and father, George and Virginia Moore; his uncles, Ernest and John Moore; and Eliza Moore, mother of George, Ernest and John, are all buried in North York's Lebanon Cemetery.

The family has roots in Bamberg, S.C.

2000: York County
Number of blacks top 10,000 in city

U.S. Census figures show that 10,270 black people live in York in 2000.

That means that blacks make up more than 25 percent of York's population. Comparable figures for 1990 were 8,968 or 21 percent; and 1980, 7,826 or 17.5 percent.

Countywide, 14,095 blacks live in 72 municipalities, making up 3.6 percent of the population in 2000.

Latinos, York's fastest-growing demographic group, more than doubled in size in the past 10 years.

In 1990, 3,244 of the city's residents were Latinos; in 2000, that number had grown to 7,026.

2000: North York
Vandals strike Lebanon Cemetery

Vandals topple 21 tombstones in Lebanon Cemetery, the historically black cemetery in North York.

Most of the damage occurs in the older part of the cemetery, where tombstones date back to the late 1800s. Two North York men are charged in connection with the incident.

The cemetery, a target of vandalism at least two other times in the past 20 years, contains markers of hundreds of people, including Civil War veterans, physicians and barbers.

In late 2001, a new flagpole and a memorial honoring all black veterans in the county are installed.

"We've got a lot of veterans buried all over York County," Thomas Montouth, a Korean War veteran, said. "This memorial is for all black veterans."

The York County Heritage Trust has located at least five other histori-

2001: York
Families of slain woman, officer meet

Hattie Dickson, facing, hugs Sharon Howe, while Sonja Gilmore, right, looks on during a meeting at the African American Love Feast in early 2002. Dickson was a sister of Allen, killed in the 1969 race riots. Gilmore was the wife of York Police Officer Henry C. Schaad, a second riot victim. Howe is Schaad's and Gilmore's daughter. This was the first public meeting of the families, who met privately a month earlier.

The families of Lillie Belle Allen and York Police Officer Henry C. Schaad meet for the first time on a cold December 2001 evening at The Yorktowne Hotel.

Allen, a black woman from South Carolina visiting relatives, had been shot and killed at the railroad tracks on North Newberry Street in York, three days after Schaad had been shot while on patrol in one of the police department's armored trucks. Schaad died in York Hospital about two weeks later. Both shootings came during the race riots that rocked York in the summer of 1969.

Earlier in 2001, prosecutors acted on grand jury recommendations when charging nine white men, including then-Mayor Charlie Robertson, in the murder of Allen. Two black men were arrested in the death of Schaad.

York County Court proceedings continue. Robertson, maintaining his innocence, is represented by a criminal defense team led by noted attorney William C. Costopoulos.

The investigation led to Robertson's withdrawal from the mayoral ballot, a spot he narrowly won over longtime city council member Ray Crenshaw in the primary.

The York County Democratic Committee picked John Brenner to replace Robertson for the Democratic ticket. Brenner beat Republican candidate Betty Schonauer and Crenshaw, a write-in candidate, for the mayor's seat in the November election.

Allen

Schaad

The Allen and Schaad families bond over the course of the 2½-hour meeting at the Yorktowne and a month later at the African American Love Feast, their first public meeting. They find many things in common.

"It was just like love spread all over us," Hattie Dickson, Lillie Belle Allen's sister, later said.

Carolyn Schaad, the deceased officer's sister-in-law, told Allen's relatives at the Love Feast, "Your family is a warm, wonderful, caring family."

cally black cemeteries in the county: Chanceford A.M.E. and Mount Olive A.M.E. cemeteries, both in Lower Chanceford Township; Mt. Zion A.M.E. in Peach Bottom Township; Stone or Mt. Pisgah Cemetery in Wrightsville; and Trinity A.M.E. Zion Cemetery in Fawn Township.

2001: York
Claiborne building officially opens

The 39,000-square-foot Loretta Claiborne Building on South George Street opens about 12 months after construction began.

The project, costing about $5 million and owned by Crispus Attucks Association, houses classrooms for Penn State York and York College; the York Hospital Community Health Center; Noah's Place, an adult day care center catering to Alzheimer's and dementia patients; and other businesses.

"All the tenants have one thing in common," Carol Kauffman, project director of Crispus Attucks, said. "They will provide goods and services to the community that were once hard to come by."

2001: York
Actors animate black history

Squire Braxton, Black Hester, William C. Goodridge and Jehu Cupit talk to residents about their lives in York in the 1800s.

Actors play these characters in "White Rose: Black Skin, The African American Presence in York County in the 1800s" before an audience at the York County Heritage Trust's Historical Society Museum.

York native Dorothy King — playwright, director, performance poet and assistant professor at Penn State Harrisburg — wrote the production. Historic writing is enjoyable, King said, because "it needs to be done."

2001: York
105-year-old matriarch passes

Ruby Ritter Jenkins, who came from the South to seek work in York County's industries in 1923, dies at the age of 105.

She was among the group who founded Bethlehem Baptist Church.

"She lived to see 19 presidents in office, Martin Luther King Jr.'s dream deferred by assassination and the birth of the Internet," a newspaper reported at the time of her death. "But more importantly, she lived to see her children grow into adults and raise families of their own."

2001: York
Hailey heads ministerial group

The Rev. Benjamin Hailey Sr., pastor of Friendship Baptist Church in York, is elected president of the Black Ministers Association of York County.

He hopes to make an impact on York in his new position, including a low-income community development credit union for working-class blacks, whites and Hispanics. His hope is that attitudes toward blacks will change.

"Only God," he said, "can change the heart." He succeeds the Rev. Aaron Willford Jr. of Bethlehem Baptist Church as head of the organization.

Hailey

2000: York
Learning life lessons

Montez Parker, right, reaches for a chess piece while playing with Luke Warner at Crispus Attucks during the after-school program.

Youth move to the boardroom to play "The Game of Life," a twice-weekly, after-school chess program at Crispus Attucks Community Center. "My focus is trying to help youth think properly. It's the thought process," Grelan Holmes, a community organizer at South George Street Community Partnership Americorps, told a newspaper. "If I can get some kids who can learn how to think through the process of chess, once they learn to strategize, and they learn they can apply it to everyday life they won't be so impulsive, and they'll learn the consequence of their actions. They will take time to look at the big picture."

2001: York
Pastor earns Love Feast honors

The Rev. William A. Johnson spearheads a national task force for urban evangelism.

He had traveled to faraway places doing missionary work. He even lived in a refugee camp in Tanzania for five weeks helping Rwandans who were crossing the border to safety.

In his 60s, he came to York to

minister at Encounter Bible Church.

Within three years, his activities in the community earn him honors at the African American Love Feast, the seventh Emmanuel Church of God in Christ-sponsored event.

Johnson joins other honorees: Ronald Banks, Wilmon Banks, Bradley Barnes, Philip Dukes, Timothy Gelzer, Joseph Jackson, Margaret Kittrell, James Morgan, Gladys Newson, Joseph Newson, Jose Pacheo, Robin Smith and Leslie Gray Streeter.

2001: York County
Poll contrasts distinct viewpoints

Two polls designed by York County's Polk-Lepson Research point to differences in views between blacks and whites.

About 63 percent of black voters in the city believe race relations have improved a lot since the 1960s, and about 43 percent believe that discrimination has decreased. Comparable responses from whites are about 85 percent and about 81 percent, respectively.

In another poll of county residents, about 23 percent of blacks said race relations are good or excellent; about 45 percent of white residents rate relations as good or excellent.

About 48 percent of blacks view race relations as fair, and 29 percent rate race relations as poor. Comparable figures for whites are about 44 percent and 12 percent, respectively.

2001: Springettsbury Township
Harley initiates diversity plan

Harley-Davidson introduces a plan to attract minority and female contractors to work on the company's proposed 350,000-square-foot expansion.

The motorcycle-maker's diverse contractor initiative is part of a company-wide program.

"It's the first serious initiative I've seen by a major corporation in central Pennsylvania," said Kerry Kirkland, a York resident and vice president of business development at the National Black Chamber of Commerce.

2002: York
Unity events coincide with clashes

Twenty-four hours after a white supremacist leader spoke at Martin Library in January 2002, friends Darnell Fitton, right, and Robert Dill hang out at the library during its Family Festival for Unity. The library had closed the day of the speech because of security concerns. It's normally closed on Sundays, but library officials put on the unity event to help the city move past the previous day's demonstrations by white supremacists and counter-protesters.

York Police arrest 23 people during a confrontation between white supremacist groups and anti-racist protesters in York.

The clashes, which send at least eight people to area hospitals with minor injuries, coincide with white supremacist Matthew Hale's visit to Martin Library. Scores of police separate the protesting groups.

At the same time, a Unity Rally Against Hate takes place at Crispus Attucks Community Center, and players compete in a five-on-five basketball tournament at Hannah Penn Middle School.

"I would like to see something like this done quarterly to remind us of the diversity of this community," the Rev. Karen House, assistant to the pastor at Friendship Baptist Church, said at Crispus Attucks. "We are actually a melting pot of different views, backgrounds and ideas, but...together we can still respond positively."

Police attempt to divide white supremacists and protesters in an attempt to prevent violence between white supremacist and anti-racist demonstrators. For a few hours on South Queen Street, police on foot and horseback created a wall and kept the groups from fighting. By the end of the day, the confrontation ended in 23 arrests.

2002: York
Ad Hoc Coalition assumes new name

The Ad Hoc Coalition takes on the more lasting name of Diversity Coalition of York County.

The coalition forms in the summer of 2001 with the temporary purpose of easing racial tensions and other community unrest stemming from arrests made in 1969 race riots murder investigations.

The name change comes as part of a January community forum — the coalition's first — to discuss the future of race relations in York.

The possible return of racist groups dominates the Diversity Coalition's first meeting.

Stephanie Seaton, city Human Relations Commission educational outreach coordinator, believes the Diversity Coalition will meet its challenges.

"We're now the Diversity Coalition of York County," she said. "I don't feel overwhelmed because it's not just for me to bear alone. We're moving away from the grass roots, and we're no longer just one person or one organization. The more people who get involved, the broader base of support we will have."

Another county group concerned about racism meets for the first time in the winter of 2002.

Eighty-five county officials, organization leaders and school personnel meet as the York County Inter-agency Task Force. The group is meeting quarterly to improve communications and share resources on race issues.

A third group meets to follow up on a YorkCounts report released in 2001, a document that measured housing, education and other issues influencing the overall well-being of the community.

These 33 community leaders, representing six groups, put forth five areas for further attention:

Addressing issues of equity in economics and racial integration; creating a countywide comprehensive strategic planning process; creating a plan for developing a more diverse work force; providing equitable educational opportunities for all York County residents; and educating the public on matters of racism and discrimination in the hopes of healing the destruction caused by both.

1990-2000s: York County
Staying in step, moving forward

The afternoon sun casts shadows, as the South Side Steppers, state drill team champions in 1993, work on their routines. The shadow of 7-year-old Burgundi Miles is the tallest. To be a member of the team, participants, ages 6-16, must achieve good grades and pass a course in female responsibility, sponsored by Youth Against Drugs.

"It's going to be up to these folks to align themselves with the groups that are involved with these issues already," Bob Woods, United Way's executive director, said. "We're hoping they are going to take a leadership role in some of these areas."

2002: York County
Black history conference

Blockson   Ham

Debra Newman Ham and Charles Blockson will be keynote speakers at the 25th Annual Conference on Black History in Pennsylvania in May.

Ham, a graduate of William Penn High School in York, is a scholar of African-American history. She is a professor at Morgan State University.

Blockson is curator of Temple University's Charles L. Blockson Afro-American Collection.

Several hundred people are expected to attend the conference. The York County Heritage Trust will play host for the three-day event, a program of the Pennsylvania Historical and Museum Commission.

A production of a play written by York native Dorothy King, an Underground Railroad exhibit at the Heritage Trust, and a Tim Warfield performance at Ruffin's jazz club in York are planned special events.

A historical marker dedication to recognize the Smallwood School is part of the schedule.

Blockson, who founded the annual event, hoped the conference would highlight York's past.

"The best history," Blockson said, "oftentimes, is local history."

Epilogue
Never to be forgotten

Solomon Washington came to York from Bamberg, S.C., upon the urging of his wife's uncle, Leon Carter. He could find a good-paying job there, Carter said, and it was a nice town. So Solomon Washington headed north as so many Bambergers had done before and since. Washington later returned to his homestead, but many Bambergers and scores of other people with southern roots decided to stay. Today, York County's black census tops 14,000 or 3.6 percent of the county's population.

We've come to the end of our photo album. Some photos are faded. Others show unidentified events needing clarification. Some photos are underexposed awaiting historians to clarify their images. Indeed, some were never taken.

The album ends with empty white pages awaiting tomorrow's snapshots.

Will photos of the future tell of our individual contributions? Will they show York County residents of all races acting out of community interests, not self-interest? Will they show a diverse community that is progressing?

One hundred years from now, will someone look through this photo album and proclaim that our best work is worthy of remembering? That our almost-forgotten achievements today should never be forgotten?

Appendix
Behind the scenes

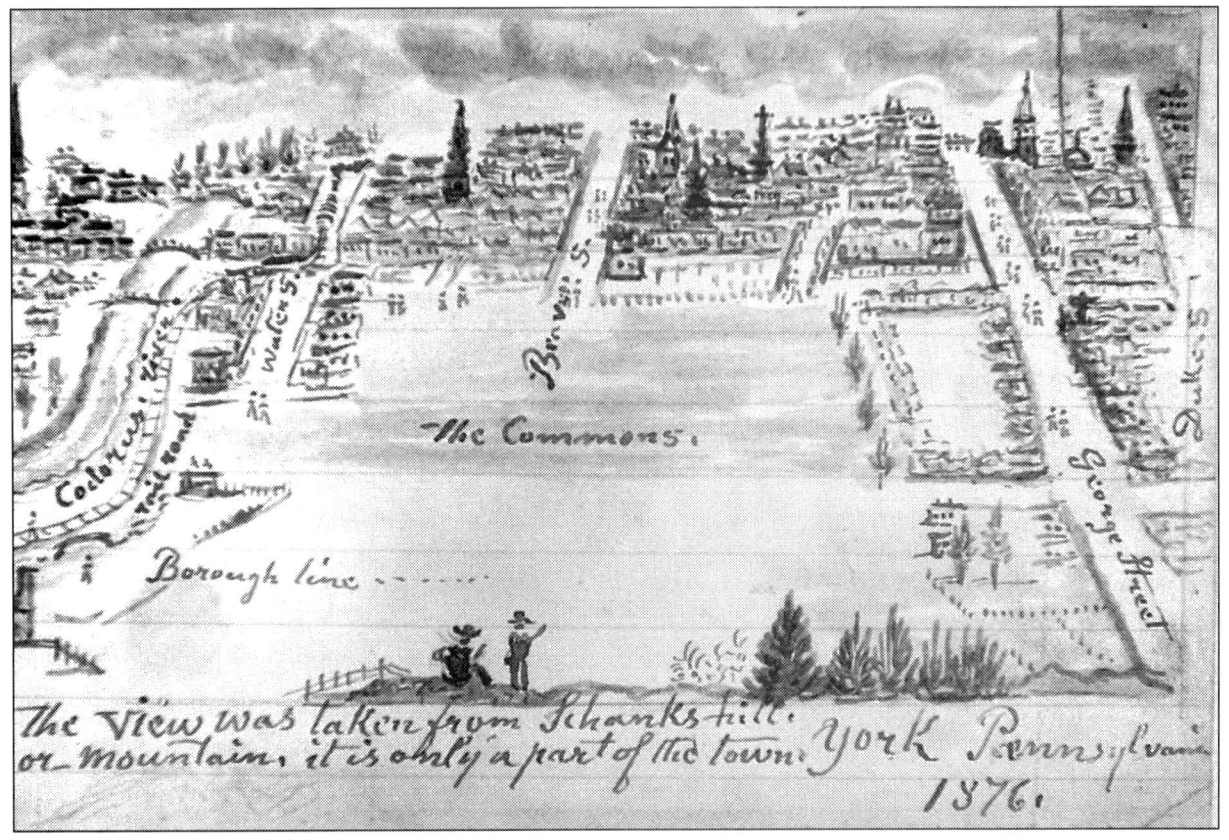

Lewis Miller captures Penn Common, now called Penn Park, in 1876. The view is from Schenk's or Shenk's Hill, called Reservoir Hill today. Through history, the park has held special significance to York County blacks.

"So many places in York County have ties with the Black Family," Jean M. Downs, wrote in a 1991 calendar spotlighting places of meaning to York County blacks. "Socially, over the years, as a total Black 'Community,' we have made much 'lemonade' from 'structural' lemons. Today housing with its growing opportunities, and the no-doors-barred policy at most local institutions are providing a changing, inclusive, socially healthier climate."

York's Penn Park was noted on the calendar as one such nostalgic site. Here, freedmen were delivered from the South to a life of liberty. Here, one of York's most colorful characters lived for decades. Here, blacks rallied to proclaim their civil rights. Here, people of all colors met to commemorate fallen leader, Dr. Martin Luther King Jr.

25 sites linked to York County's black heritage

Several members of York County's black community helped develop a calendar in connection with the City of York's 250th anniversary in 1991. The calendar featured a sampling of photographs and descriptions of sites around York that held special meaning to many in the black community. Edited and updated versions of the descriptions appear at right.

Jean M. Downs, committee member, wrote the following in a prologue:

"Respectfully, in retrospect, we mention the 'remembered' physical area — now gone — Princess Street west from George Street to the bridge. Those blocks housed many Black-owned businesses: restaurants, shops, stores, organizations serving the African-American community. Our young people are not always aware of the successful enterprises once there. Do tell them!

"On this calendar all of the meaningful sites could not possibly be included. This printed effort is to honor, to stimulate and to allow you to recall pleasantly the places herein."

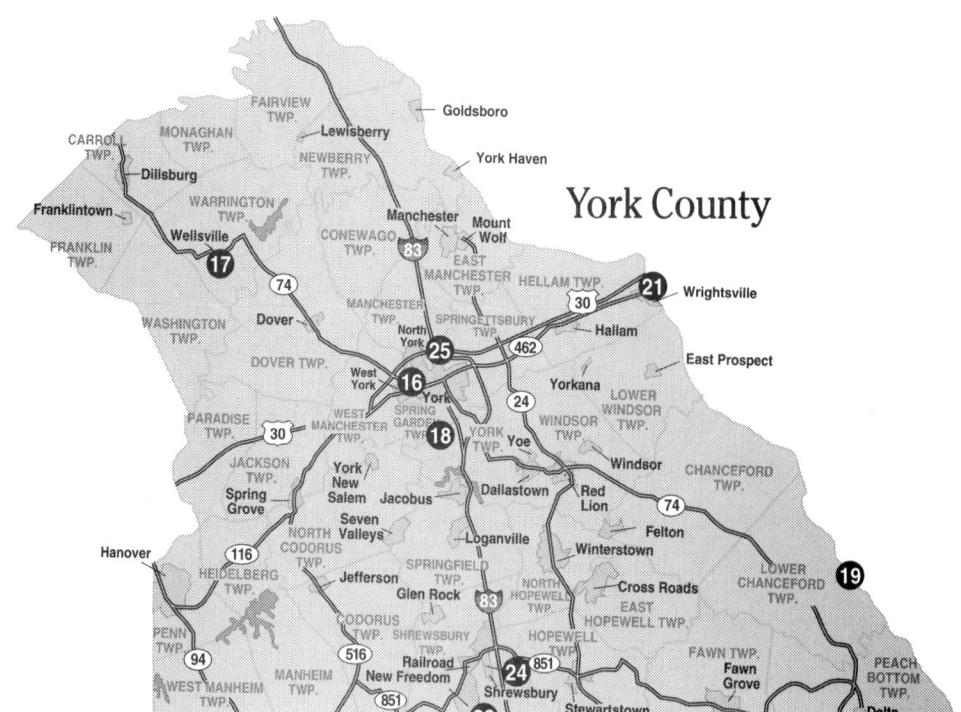

York County

1. The Valencia Ballroom for years was off-limits to the black population. This is interesting because many "Big Band" members that played there were black. These members had to depend on local black boarding homes for food and lodging as York's restaurants and hotels were also off-limits. Note that, for a short period in 1959, William "Brice" Jackson and LaFair "Jimmy" Horton from the black community, operated the Valencia's Rainbow Grill as a restaurant.

2. The older part of the York Meeting House was erected in 1766 at 135 W. Philadelphia St. by the Society of Friends. In York County the principal helpers on the "Underground Railroad" were Quakers. The York Meeting House, which was enlarged in 1783, was the site of many anti-slavery sessions.

3a-3b. William C. Goodridge was in the barber business and also sold candy, toys and newspapers. In 1847, he built York's first five-story building, "Centre Hall." His sons were professional photographers. His home was in the 100 block of East Philadelphia Street, at the spot of the historic marker. His home and "Centre Hall" are both associated with the Underground Railroad. York City Councilman Wm. Lee Smallwood aided in gaining the marker.

4. Penn Park, or Penn Common, is remembered with nostalgia by York's black families. It was a delightful, recreational meeting site over the years. York history states that, on one moonlit night in May 1827, two wagons carrying 52 free Negroes came into York from near Leesburg and Alexandria, Va. A Quaker, Jesse Kersey, unloaded the freedmen on Penn Common and pleaded to local citizens to provide housing and jobs for them. One of the freedmen, Squire Braxton, spent all of his days in a self-made shanty on Penn Common.

5. Most black families arriving in York in the 1920s and 1930s found housing near the Codorus Creek in the west end of the city — Newberry, Princess, King, Codorus and Allison streets along with College Avenue and the many intersecting alleys. Today, the same area is hailed as a redeveloped, revitalized, integrated community.

6. The Cookes House, located at the Codorus Creek adjoining Penn Street, is a gray fieldstone house built in 1761. Legend has long held that Thomas Paine stayed in the house when visiting York with Congress in 1777-78, but that claim has not been documented. In much later years, before undergoing renovations by Historic York Inc., the building housed the Hunter and Hughes families and other black residents.

7. The floods of 1933 and 1972 were especially devastating to many black families, who were housed so near to the Codorus. They were easily surrounded by the overflowing, rushing waters.

8. The Barnett Bobb House in its early years lists Yorkers of note as its inhabitants. Also, prior to its relocation to Pershing Avenue at the rear of Market Street, it housed a number of black families and a black-owned fish market.

9. The Yorktowne Hotel, at the corner of Duke and Market streets, was built in 1925. Since then, it has been York's most elegant hotel. From the beginning, its more-than-qualified black employees built the hotel's reputation. Two early hotel waiters, Mr. Russell and Mr. Pittman, were college graduates.

10. York Manufacturing Company, now York International, was one of the earliest employers of African-Americans migrating to York County in the 1920s and 1930s. The present-day York

County Industrial Plaza occupies York Manufacturing Company's former site. York International, successor to York Manufacturing and Borg-Warner, operates from a Spring Garden Township site.

11a.-11b. Smallwood and Aquilla Howard schools, west and east of downtown, were built to accommodate the overflow of students of new families arriving in York in the 1920s and 1930s. Henry Hopewell was the well-known principal to "Smallwooders." Anna Mead Dabney was principal at Aquilla Howard. Both were strong school heads, recognized in the community for their leadership. Later, shortly before school integration in the 1950s, Charles Grayson was Smallwood's principal.

12. The Crispus Attucks Community Center was located in the old York Hospital building at College Avenue and the Codorus Creek bridge. When the hospital moved to the hill on South George Street, the building was acquired for the black community through the efforts of black physician George W. Bowles. He sought Chester N. Hayes, an out-of-towner, to direct the center. Many of York's bounty of early college graduates — Bill Hunter, Eenio Miller, Tillman Sease, Mel Ransom, William Myers, Lois Lambert, Henry Nimmons, "Abe" Ritter, Carrie Palmer Ford and so many others — were motivated and nurtured there. In its early years, Clarence Jackson Sr. provided ice cream and candy at a confectionery location on the center's second floor.

13. The Armory Building, on North George Street at the Codorus Creek bridge, was rented on several occasions by Mahlon N. Haines, the "Shoe Wizard." He knew of the limited social facilities of the black community in the 1930s and 1940s, so he, at these free affairs, provided live bands and plenty of food. Haines also insisted on integrated Boy and Girl Scouts celebrations at his eastern York County Wizard Ranch so he could include the still-segregated Scout units.

14. The now-demolished Duke Street Market, also known as the City Market, stood near Princess Street, next door to the corner A&P store. It was a busy hub on market days. In the 1930s and 1940s, neighborhood black and white youths, with their red wagons and regular customers, delivered brimming baskets directly to homes for a fee. Competition, camaraderie and "business experience and sense" provided them with sizable earnings on Saturdays.

15. York Collegiate Institute, a forerunner of York College, and a "private" school, was on Duke Street, adjacent to the Duke Street Market. When the school moved to its new site, the building was torn down to become

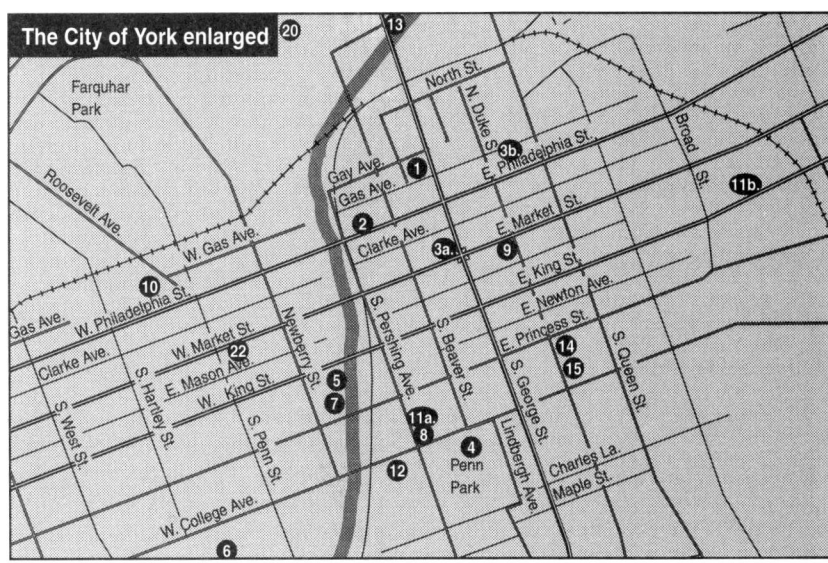

Campus Park, a "public" city playground. Looking to the rear of the school, its gym still stands. This is now known as Voni B. Grimes Gym. The now-demolished Smallwood and Aquilla Howard schools had previously been named for black Yorkers. Other York buildings named after blacks include: the Loretta Claiborne Building, part of the Boundary Avenue project at South George Street, which opened in 2001; the Charles E. Williams American Legion Post on East Princess Street and the Goodridge Business Resource Center in the York County Industrial Plaza.

16. The York Fairgrounds is certainly one of the few locations having always had its facilities open to the total community. African-American families, like everyone else, have enjoyed years of fun at the York Fair. From time to time, black entertainers of national fame have been booked for the grandstand.

Underground Railroad sites*

17. Fugitive slaves traveling from "stations" in Adams County found refuge among the Quakers of Warrington Meeting. They traveled on to cross the Susquehanna River at Middletown Ferry, Dauphin County.

18. Springwood Farm is located south of York on the Old Baltimore Pike. The Jessop and Chalfant families provided food to runaway slaves who were hidden under the hay in their barns.

19. After crossing the Susquehanna River at McCall's Ferry in Lower Chanceford Township, fugitive slaves followed routes eastward through Lancaster County to Christiana and on to Philadelphia.

20. The Willis farm is situated north of the city at the foot of Prospect Hill. While the house and barn undoubtedly afforded shelter, one account tells of fugitive slaves being hidden inside corn shocks in the adjoining fields.

21. Fugitive slaves crossed the Wrightsville Bridge undetected, hidden in railroad cars owned by William C. Goodridge. Some were rowed across the river by friendly boatmen.

Other sites

22. A mural, near West Market and South Penn streets, shows a larger-than-life William C. Goodridge standing before some of his accomplishments — his building devoted to various business lines, barbershop and a rail line. The mural also shows Goodridge as an infant son of a slave and then as a boy beginning his indenture.

23. The Mason-Dixon Line, bordering York County on the south, was run by the famous British surveying team from 1763-1767. The county's position on this dividing line between North and South, free and slave states, drew residents into abolitionist controversies of the day. The county's proximity to the Mason-Dixon Line also meant its residents developed many business, cultural and social ties to the South.

24. A marker near the former Grace United Methodist Church in Shrewsbury designates where Amanda Berry Smith, a nationally prominent missionary and singer, was converted to Christianity. Smith was born a slave in Maryland, and her family moved to a farm near Shrewsbury when she was young.

25. Lebanon Cemetery is the largest of about a half dozen known historically black cemeteries in York County. Many prominent black York County residents are buried in this North York cemetery.

*Descriptions from York County Heritage Trust.

22 Profiles in Heritage: A celebration of York County's black history

To document the accomplishments of black people in history, the York Daily Record published profiles of 25 achievers from a host of people connected to York County who have made a difference locally, statewide or nationally in the 20th and 21st century. A digest of 22 of those profiles, appearing in the winter and spring of 2002, is published here.

Marie White Bell

Marie White Bell

Occupation: State Superior Court Judge in New Jersey
Birthplace: York
Current home: Springfield Township, in New Jersey
Education: Bachelor's degree in biology from Lycoming College in Williamsport; and law degree from Seton Hall University in East Orange, N.J.
Background: Residents of Willingboro, Burlington County, N.J., elected Bell as their first black mayor in 1980. She worked 12 years as a biologist, while attending law school at night. She later worked as a New Jersey municipal court judge for 17 years before taking a seat on the Superior Court.
Best advice? Marie White Bell: "Never forget where you came from."

Wade Hampton Bowers III

Occupation: Retired as director of music and educational activities at the Crispus Attucks Community Center
Born: Sept. 28, 1905
Birthplace: Savannah, Ga.
Died: May 8, 1993

Wade Hampton Bowers III

Education: Received a bachelor's degree in music theory from Morehouse College in Atlanta, Ga.
Memories about Bowers: Julia Hines-Harris, longtime teacher and administrator in the York City School District, provides this assessment:
"When we sang, he made it our calling. I can still remember many of the songs we used to sing. We sang in Italian and in other languages. We sang songs from operas. He gave us songs that carried us through. He demanded that we get the best and be the best that we could be."

George Bowles

George Bowles

Occupation: Physician
Born: 1871
Birthplace: Unknown
Died: Oct. 8, 1951
Education: 1898 graduate of York High School; 1902 graduate from Livingstone College in Salisbury, N.C.; and, in 1906, received his medical degree from Howard University Medical School in Washington, D.C.
Bowles' influence on York County: "Everyone looked up to him," York resident Voni B. Grimes said. "If Dr. Bowles said something, people listened. Because he was a black doctor, young men and women from the black community looked up to him. Most people, even whites, knew Dr. Bowles."

Mattie Chapman

Mattie Chapman

Occupation: Prothonotary
Born: Feb. 24, 1927
Birthplace: Albany, Ga.
Died: June 13, 1982
Education: Graduated from Albany State College with business degree.
Background: Chapman was the first black person elected to a York County office.
Best advice? Chapman told others to trust in God and treat people with respect and dignity — even if they don't treat you that way, York County Prothonotary Stacia Gates said.

W. Russell Chapman and Mildred Chapman

W. Russell Chapman

Occupation: W. Russell Chapman, funeral director; and Mildred Chapman, director of the Women and Girls Program at the Crispus Attucks Community Center. W. Russell Chapman was the first black member of the York City School Board.
Born: W. Russell Chapman, 1898; Mildred Chapman, 1904.

Birthplace: W. Russell Chapman was born in Uniontown, Fayette County, and Mildred Chapman was born in Oklahoma.
Dates of death: W. Russell Chapman died in January 1971. Mildred Chapman died in January 1987.

Mildred Chapman

Education: W. Russell Chapman graduated from Howard University with a bachelor's degree and from Cornell University with a master's degree. He went on to Colan's College of Embalming School in Chicago and the University of Wisconsin. Mildred Chapman graduated from Howard University with a degree in pharmaceutical chemistry.
Impact on their professions: York resident Alice Bowers: "Anything that was good for people, she (Mildred Chapman) was behind it. She was always pushing people to achieve as much as they could achieve."

"Mr. Chapman wouldn't turn people away (even if they didn't have the money to bury their loved ones). He taught people how to help others in spite of money."

Joseph Douglas

Occupation: Retired from Penn State, Capital Campus, as an electrical engineering professor. He also taught engineering at Penn State York.
Born: Oct. 31, 1926
Birthplace: Indianapolis, Ind.
Current home: Springettsbury Township
Education: Bachelor's degree in electrical engineering from Purdue University in West Lafayette, Ind.; master's degree in electrical engineering from University of Missouri.
What makes a hero? Joseph Douglas: "A hero is one who is held at high esteem by an admirer for the types of things he or she does and the unselfish manner in which those things are done. And, often a hero is successful at what is being attempted. You can be a hero and fail at it, but at least you've attempted it."

Joseph Douglas

Carrie Ford

Occupation: Retired as teacher from Hannah Penn Middle School in 1972 and worked as a missionary for 17 years.
Born: Sept. 11, 1910
Birthplace: Greensboro, N.C.
Died: Jan. 25, 2001
Education: Bachelor's degree from Livingstone College with a certificate to teach language arts; also attended Millersville State Teachers College and York Collegiate Institute.
Background: Known to many as Mother Ford, Carrie Ford dedicated her life to helping others. She taught French at York City schools before she retired in 1972. That same year, at age 62, she flew to Liberia and began to teach children English and the Word of God. She spent 17 years there, teaching, building homes and schools, and spreading the Gospel.
Carrie Ford's contribution to York County and the world: "She affected the world by the (missionary) work she did in Liberia," her daughter, Diane Scott, said. "Locally, she was a role model for many people, especially the children she taught. Everyone looked up to her."

Carrie Ford

Voni B. Grimes

Occupation: Retired from Penn State York as director of business services.
Born: Dec. 23, 1922
Birthplace: Bamberg, S.C.

Voni B. Grimes

Current home: York
Education: Graduate of William Penn Senior High School. Attended Penn State York, York College and the University of Kentucky.
Best advice? Voni B. Grimes: "Stay in school and get an education. It's better to have the education and not need it than to need it and not have it. Should you have it, you should make a contribution to your community rather than just being a number in your community."

Debra Newman Ham

Occupation: History professor at Morgan State University in Baltimore
Born: Aug. 27, 1948
Birthplace: York
Current home: Laurel, Md.
Education:

Debra Newman Ham

Bachelor's degree in history from Howard University; master's degree in African history from Boston University; doctorate in African history from Howard University.
Best advice? Debra Newman Ham: "This is a quote, I don't know whose it is: 'God gives his best to those who leave the choice with him.'"

Ernie Hartzog

Occupation: After 20 years of service, Hartzog retired in 1992 as associate superintendent of the Portland, Ore., school district.
Born: Jan. 8, 1928
Birthplace: York
Current home: Portland, Ore.

Ernie Hartzog

Education: Bachelor's degree in education from San Diego State University in San Diego, Calif.; master's degree in education from San Diego State University; master's degree in counseling psychology from New York University; doctorate in psy-

chology and human behavior from United States International University in San Diego.
Best advice: Ernie Hartzog: "Learn to believe in yourself in a positive way. I feel if I can love myself and feel positive about myself it is much easier to love other people."

Julia Hines-Harris

Julia Hines-Harris

Occupation: Retired July 2001, after 36 years in the York City School District. Her last position was assistant superintendent for secondary education.
Born: Oct. 20, 1940
Birthplace: York
Current home: Springettsbury Avenue, York
Education: Graduated from William Penn Senior High School in 1958; graduated from Cheyney State College with bachelor's of science degree in education and a minor in special education; earned a master's degree from Millersville University; and received doctorate in education from the University of Pennsylvania.
What makes a hero? Julia Hines-Harris: "Not so much what they say, but what they do — and the reasons they do it. Heroes don't seek fame and fortune. If it comes for them, heroes usually pass the spotlight and fame off to other people.

"Heroes aren't only people who climb mountains or go to the moon or do those daring things, but heroes are keepers of the heart."

Dorothy King

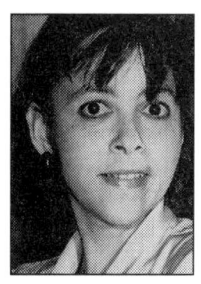
Dorothy King

Occupation: Assistant professor of behavioral sciences education and humanities at Penn State Harrisburg
Birthplace: York
Current home: Harrisburg
Education: Bachelor's degree in early childhood education from Temple University in Philadelphia; master's degree in early childhood education from New York University; master's of education in family and community education from Teachers College, Columbia University in New York.
What is your inspiration? Dorothy King: "I am inspired by my belief that we all have a purpose. I believe that God has sent us here to make life a little better for each other and to take care of the earth. Writing is my contribution. That's what inspires me."

The Rev. Leslie Lawson

The Rev. Leslie Lawson

Occupation: He worked as a clergyman at Camp Hill Correctional Institution counseling people. But he left there to go into full-time ministry. He retired after 23 years of service at Small Memorial A.M.E. Zion Church, 401 S. Queen St., York, in 1992.
Born: May 5, 1923
Birthplace: Jamaica, West Indies
Died: June 17, 1998
Education: Attended University of West Indies, Yale Divinity School and University of Maine. Lawson had a bachelor's degree, master's of divinity degree and doctorate.
Background: Lawson marched with the Rev. Dr. Martin Luther King Jr., and he was jailed with him for five days after praying on the steps of an Atlanta courthouse in 1962.
A.M.E. Zion Bishop Milton A. Williams Sr. eulogized Lawson: "Leslie G. Lawson, a minister of the Gospel, a brother, a friend, a wonderful man, was invested with talents," Williams said. "He invested his life and his talents in bringing liberation and freedom to people. He invested his talents in the marketplace of human needs."

The Rev. Richard Manning

The Rev. Richard Manning

Occupation: Longtime pastor of York's Shiloh Baptist Church and current pastor of St. John Baptist Church in Reading for the past 18 years.
Born: Aug. 15, 1918
Birthplace: Cherokee County, S.C.
Current home: 130 W. Maple Street, York
Education: Attended Franklin Institute in Rochester, N.Y., and Maryland Theological Seminary at Morgan State University. Received bachelor's of theology degree from the American Bible College of Pineland, Ind., and a degree from the Pioneer Theological Seminary of Rockland, Ind.
Quotable: Daughter Marilyn Manning remembers Richard Manning's counsel: "My dad would always say two things: 'Put God first in all that you do.' Then he would say, 'I serve a living God, haven't you read? He's a God of the living, not of the dead.'"

Robert C. Maynard

Robert C. Maynard

Occupation: Robert C. Maynard arrived at his first newspaper job at The York Gazette and Daily in 1961. By 1968, he was at The Washington Post covering the riots following Dr. Martin Luther King Jr.'s assassination and the White House during the Vietnam War. He later purchased The Oakland Tribune, the first black to own a major metropolitan newspaper.
Born: 1937
Died: 1993
Birthplace: Brooklyn, N.Y.
Education: Maynard was a high school dropout. "My credentials," he

said at the time, "will be my work." He later was awarded eight honorary degrees, including one from York College in 1984.

Maynard's view of York: "As you can see, the old local joke goes, give or take a few miles and York ... might have been one heck of a town. Right off, I'll admit my prejudice. I happen to think it is one heck of a town without being any closer than it is to some of its famous neighbors."

Maynard's view of racism: Daughter Dori J. Maynard recalls: "The summer I discovered racism, the kind of 'I don't need to know you to hate you' racism, my father called me and said: 'Racism is someone else's sickness. You must never let it infect you. You must not let it change who you are.'"

Maynard's optimism: "The country's greatest achievements came about because somebody believed in something, whether it was in a steam engine, an airplane or a space shuttle. Only when we lose hope in great possibilities are we really doomed. Reversals and tough times inspire some people to work harder for what they believe in."

Daisy Myers

Occupation: Daisy Myers spent 20 years working with children in York City schools. She retired as principal of Arthur W. Ferguson Elementary in 1980, then worked for 17 years in the York office of then-U.S. Rep. Bill Goodling, R-York County.
Born: Feb. 10, 1925
Birthplace: Richmond, Va.
Current home: York Township
Education: Bachelor's degree from Virginia Union University and master's degree from Purdue University, both in psychology.
Background: She and her late husband, William, who died in 1987, broke the color line by purchasing a home in all-white Levittown, Bucks County, in August 1957.
The move unleashed a mob of protesters. Despite this opposition, the Myerses remained in their home. Several years later, the Myerses moved to a York County subdivision where they were well received.

Best advice? "Look for the good in people," Daisy Myers said, comparing it to a rose garden. "A garden of red roses is beautiful, but a garden of mixed roses — red, yellow, white and pink is more beautiful. We need to stop and smell all the roses."

Daisy Myers

David Orr

Occupation: Associate pastor at Shiloh Baptist Church and owner of Fisher Refuse Collection Co.
Born: July 27, 1902
Died: May 3, 1973
Birthplace: Bamberg, S.C.
Education: Eighth-grade education in South Carolina.
Background: Orr and his wife, the former Eula Mae Nimmons, built the trash collection business into a company that serviced many residences and commercial interests in the York area.
Best advice? "As a deeply religious man and humanitarian, Rev. Orr counseled others to have faith in God and in themselves and to live their lives without anger or without bitterness," his daughter, M.K. Orr, said. "That's something he said often."

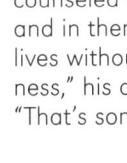
David Orr

William Ransom

Occupation: William Ransom, who grew up in York, retired in 1979 as an administrator in the Coatesville Area School District, Pa.
Born: March 15, 1914
Birthplace: Bamberg County, S.C.
Current home: Gloucester County, Va.
Education: Graduated in 1937 with a bachelor's degree in secondary education from Lincoln University; received master's degree in school administration from Temple University.
Best advice? William Ransom: "Go to school, trust in God and study hard. Get ready, someday your chance will come."

William Ransom

Tillman Sease

Occupation: Tillman Sease, who grew up in York, was the chairman of the Department of Health and Physical Education and assistant coach in football and basketball and head coach in baseball at Bluefield State College in West Virginia. ("They had one person do the whole nine yards then," said one of his sons, Tillman Sease Jr.) Later, he moved to Howard University, retiring from coaching in 1974.
Born: Sept. 6, 1916
Died: Sept. 2, 1988
Birthplace: Bamberg, S.C.
Education: Bachelor's degree in physical education/health and recreation from Bluefield State College in Bluefield, W.V.; master's degree in education from Columbia University, N.Y.

Tillman Sease

What should York County residents know about Sease? York resident Vincent Barnes, another son: "The fact that ... he led by example. He went out and didn't just talk about something, he did it. To me, it seemed like he lived life to the max. He enjoyed what he was doing and he did it well."

James Sexton

James Sexton

Occupation: James Sexton, who grew up in York, retired from the law firm of Robert Sexton & Moultrie in Washington, D.C., which specializes in entrepreneurial and domestic international business.
Born: Sept. 1, 1927
Birthplace: Bamberg, S.C.
Current home: Silver Spring, Md.
Education: Received a bachelor's degree in economics and political science from Howard University in Washington, D.C.; received a degree from Georgetown Law School in Washington, D.C.
Best advice? James Sexton: "The best piece I can give is think for yourself and be yourself. The best piece of advice that I can give is a poem: Do the dance you've been shown, by everyone you've known, until the dance becomes your every own, into a dancer you've grown, from seeds someone else has thrown, go ahead throw some seeds of your own, somewhere between the time you arrive and the time you go home, because in the end there is one dance you will do alone."

Helen L. Thackston

Helen L. Thackston

Occupation: Director of the day care program, Crispus Attucks Community Center
Born: 1891
Birthplace: York
Died: 1969
Thackston's impact on York County: Ray Crenshaw, former York city councilman who thought of Thackston as a mother, provides this assessment:

"She affected the York community really from an educational standpoint. It was something that transcended the black community because of her efforts. A number of people from the majority community got to know her and they supplied her and the kids at the CA with numerous things: clothing, shoes for kids who were without them, Christmas parties, Easter egg hunts during that time and items for Girls Scouts. It was beyond just one community. It transcended the whole city because everyone knew her."

Reuben Washington

Reuben Washington

Occupation: Since 1980, Washington has been in solo, private practice as an orthopedic surgeon in the Rochester, N.Y., area.
Born: Oct. 1, 1942
Birthplace: Floala, Ala.
Current home: Rochester, N.Y.
Family background: He had eight siblings.
Education: Graduated from William Penn High School in York, class of 1961, where he was a championship wrestler; received bachelor's of science degree in pre-medicine from Lincoln University in Oxford, Pa.; graduated from Yale University in New Haven, Conn., in 1971 with a graduate degree in public health; received degree in medicine from the University of Pittsburgh in 1975.
Best advice: Reuben Washington?: "I think, you know, it goes back to my parents. I think we were all raised to do our best and to try to improve ourselves and to make the most of what we have and the opportunities that we had. I think if I was going to give any advice it would be don't give up on a dream — however remote. Because if you work toward that dream or goal, most likely you will succeed more times than not."

12 questions and answers about York County's black heritage

See answers on Page 78.

Helen L. Thackston

Aunt Jo

Ella J. Robinson, one of the pioneering teachers at Smallwood School.

1. William Russell Chapman was appointed to serve the rest of an unexpired term to elective office. What was his position and when did he serve?
  A: City School Board, 1954-1956
  B: City School Board, 1967-1971
  C: York County Commissioner, 1970-1974
  D: York County Prothonotary, 1976-1980

2. In the City of York, a small park off College Avenue is named in memory of Helen L. Thackston. Why?
  A: She gave the city the land.
  B: Her home was on the site of the park.
  C: She helped care for and educate inner-city children all her life.
  D: She taught black children at a school once on the site.

3. The Supreme Court ordered the desegregation of all public schools in its Brown vs. Board of Education decision. While the high school in York had long been integrated, the elementary schools generally were not. Black students typically attended Smallwood and Aquilla Howard elementary schools. Upon request, some black students could attend other elementary schools as space was available. What decade did the Supreme Court decision spurring integration come down?
  A: 1920s   B: 1930s
  C: 1940s   D: 1950s

4. This 19th-century artist painted the everyday people of York, both black and white?
  A: Horace Bonham
  B: William Wagner
  C: Squire Braxton
  D: Washington Dorsey

5. Which of the following is a historically black cemetery?
  A: Prospect Hill Cemetery
  B: Lebanon Cemetery
  C: Mount Rose Cemetery
  D: Moravian Cemetery

6. Pennsylvania was the first state in the union to pass a law calling for the gradual abolition of slavery. When was it passed?
  A: 1825   B: 1800
  C: 1780   D: 1857

7. When is it believed that the last person to be a slave in York County died?
  A: 1841   B: 1790
  C: 1860   D: 1900

8. In the first half of the 20th century, this black physician was considered the "mayor" of the black community. What was his name?
  A: Aquilla Howard
  B: George Bowles
  C: James Smallwood
  D: Squire Braxton

9. Who was both the first black hired for a county office and elected to a county office?
  A: Mattie Chapman
  B: Aquilla Howard
  C: Emily Goodridge
  D: Helen L. Thackston

10. Who was Aunt Jo and why was a city street, Aunt Jo Lane, named for her in 1980?
  A: She operated a bakery on the spot and often gave children special discounts on doughnuts.
  B: She took in homeless children and they called her Aunt Jo.
  C: A Girl Scout leader for years, she was loved by the children in her neighborhood.
  D: She gave free music lessons to gifted children.

11. Who was Crispus Attucks?
  A: A black leader in York
  B: A civil rights activist
  C: An 18th-century man living in Boston
  D: A professional football player

12. What Wrightsville native became secretary of the New York YMCA?
  A. John Wright
  B. Susanna Wright
  C. James Barton
  D. James L. Jamison Jr.

It is boys against girls during a May festival at Smallwood School in 1956. The girls beat the boys in this circus relay. Carol Carter was festival queen and Beverly Boanes and Barbara Duke, her attendants. The Brown vs. Board of Education decision expedited integration of York's schools.

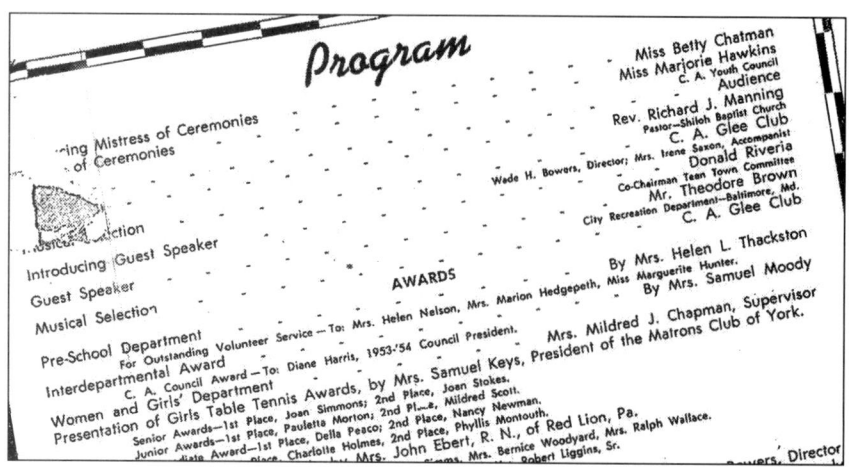

This worn Crispus Attucks Association Awards Program gives a sampling of activities at the center as well as those in leadership positions at the center in the 1950s. Some of the awards and presenters follow: meritorious awards, Mrs. John Ebert, Red Lion; education department, Wade Hampton Bowers; pocket billiards, Donald J. Cockley; physical education department, Jack B. Cornette; Eastern Pennsylvania Recreation Association, Edward R. Simmons; and physical committee, Dr. O.H. Kimbrough. Crispus Attucks Association was named after the first man to die for America's freedom.

Answers

1. B: Mr. Chapman was a York mortician respected for his interest in helping the community. He was appointed to the city school board in 1967 and elected in 1969. Because of his ill health, some meetings were held at his funeral home. Mr. Chapman died in 1971.

2. C: After the Crispus Attucks Community Center was established in 1931, Helen L. Thackston started its preschool program and served as its director until 1964. She also headed the young people's choir at her church and was superintendent of its Sunday school for the primary grades. For the first 15 years, she worked without pay. Her care for the children in the preschool program at Crispus Attucks included meeting the children at Penn Park and walking them to and from Crispus Attucks. She died in 1969, and the park was named for her in 1972.

3. D: In the Brown vs. Board of Education decision in 1954, the two black elementary schools began to be phased out, and integration of public elementary schools was accelerated.

4. A: Horace Bonham was known to portray blacks in his paintings, which was unusual for the time period. These paintings help to provide a picture about the life of 19th-century blacks in York.

5. B: Even burial grounds were segregated by race. The Lebanon Cemetery in North York was established as a black cemetery and continues to be used that way today.

6. C: In 1780, a measure was passed for gradual abolition of slavery. Pennsylvania was the first state in the union to pass an abolition law.

7. A: The last slave died in 1841. His name isn't known, but a family named Forney in Hanover owned him.

8. B: For much of the time he was in practice, Dr. George Bowles was York's only black doctor.

9. A: Mrs. Chapman began her career in government as a clerk in the prothonotary office in York County Courthouse in 1956. In 1975, she ran and won the office of prothonotary. She ran again in 1979 and won the post by a landslide. Her term was cut short by her death in 1982.

10. C: Joanna Harris was active in the formation of Girl Scout troops in downtown York and was known as "Aunt Jo." A street in her neighborhood was named in her honor after her death.

11. C: Before the outbreak of the Revolutionary War, Crispus Attucks was among those protesting the tea tax. British soldiers killed him. Crispus Attucks, son of an African man, became the first to die for America's freedom. The Crispus Attucks Association in York bears his name.

12. D. James L. Jamison, Jr., son of a long-time Wrightsville physician, graduated as valedictorian of his class from Wrightsville High School in 1902. He graduated magna cum laude from Lincoln University in 1906, took graduate courses from Rutgers College in 1912-1914 and served as a school principal in Carlisle, Pa.; Frostburg, Md.; Sumerville, N.J.; and Princeton, N.J. Jamison was in great demand as a public speaker. "There is no question that Mr. Jamison has attained more credit than any graduate of his race from our school or Lincoln University," a 1916 Wrightsville High School alumni book states. "Keep up the good work; we wish you success."

9 months in York Town: Slaves included in Continental Congress' visit

Slavery was legal throughout the United States during the early years of the American Revolution.

The issue was never far from the minds of those sitting in Continental Congress in York Town, present-day York, for a nine-month period, Sept. 30, 1777-June 27, 1778. They dealt with the issue on several different levels — in their deliberations in the York County Court House, in their correspondence and in the management of their personal servants. Meanwhile, county residents took advantage of the Pennsylvania Gazette, publishing between Dec. 20 and June 20 in York Town, to sell and track their slaves.

These stories from "Nine Months in York Town" relate how slaves and slavery issues were a regular public topic during Congress' visit in 1777-78.

From their earliest days in York Town, delegates talked among themselves about the improbability of America gaining foreign aid from France, Spain and other countries without a document showing that the 13 Colonies had agreed to work together.

Congress took up debate on the Articles of Confederation on its eighth day in York Town — Oct. 7.

Money and taxes — the basis on which states should pay into a common fund — dominated early debate. The original draft of the Articles said states were to pay taxes in proportion to their total number of inhabitants, including slaves. Some delegates followed Maryland delegate Samuel Chase's argument that slaves were property and, thus, should not be subject to taxation. The Northern farmer invested in livestock, and the southern planter bought and fed slaves. Livestock would not be taxed, so why slaves?

Whether labor is free or via servitude makes no difference, John Adams and others countered. It is the number of laborers that produces the surplus for taxation.

This topic of taxation angered Henry Laurens, the slaveholding South Carolina delegate.

"…(S)ome sensible things have been said, & as much nonsense as ever I heard in so short a space, I have not contributed to either," Laurens wrote his son, John. "I mean to expose my inabilities this Morning in a very few words because I think few are necessary…."

• • •

A calm Richard Henry Lee of Virginia, not the opinionated Henry Laurens, presented the decisive argument. Lee saw that division, split among northern free states and southern slaveholding states, would deter union and impair the fight for freedom.

"…(I)n this great business… we must yield a little to each other, and not rigidly insist on having everything correspondent to the partial views of every state," he argued. "On such terms, we can never confederate."

He pointed to history. Wealth was connected with the value of land, not with the number of people residing on a property.

Lee was willing to give. His home state of Virginia would pay more if taxes were based on land rather than on people. But that was the fairest basis for taxation. Lee's idea won. Five states voted yes, four no.

Taxation would be based on the value of all land within each state, and the buildings and improvements would be estimated according to rules of Congress.

One hundred and fifty years later, the writer of a proclamation celebrating

Young Phyllis Wheatley, a former slave and poet who caught George Washington's attention, optimistically writes in 1772 that Britain's new North American secretary would be supportive of black and white colonists: 'No more America, in mournful strain/Of wrongs, and grievance unredress'd complain/No longer shalt thou dread the iron chain/Which wanton Tyranny with lawless hand/Had made, and with it meant t' enslave the land.'

Congress' visit points out the significance of the body's vote on taxation: "Here… the Representatives in Congress struck from the quick a vital spark. They refused absolutely to tax the negro man either as a chattle or a slave. Had Congress done less than that, America could not have become the Leader of Freedom among the Nations of the World. That latent spark, sealed for four and eighty years, thereafter flashed into a corrosive flame — then self-consumed — expired forever."

• • •

Cornelius Harnett, a mercantilist before the war, paused from his duties to write to his friend, William Wilkinson, about business. The war was forcing up prices, the North Carolina delegate wrote. Rum. Slaves. Other commodities.

"…(Y)ou may be Assured you may purchase Negroes or any other Article of Commerce 150 per Cent Cheaper in No. Carolina than you could in Philadelphia before Congress left it," he advised.

"500 dollars for a small Mulatto boy has

American history remembers the Boston Massacre because the first blood of the American Revolution was spilled on a March evening in 1770. Five Americans died that day, including Crispus Attucks, said to be an offspring of an African man and a Nantucket Indian mother. Attucks took two shots in the chest, the first of the protesters to die. Attucks, believed to be a runaway slave, joined a group of youths and men who threw snowballs at a British soldier guarding the custom house. The British authorities had enflamed the public, trying to enforce new tax laws. A squad of redcoats arrived on the scene and opened fire on the protesters. The patriots immediately tagged the shootings as 'The Boston Massacre,' and Attucks and four others killed that night became martyrs. John Adams successfully defended the eight British soldiers in court, describing Attucks as the self-appointed leader of 'the dreadful carnage.'

been lately given.

"As to Labourers, you may surely get them either on purchase or hire 100 per Cent Cheaper than I can possibly procure them here."

• • •

News of a slave desertion from one of his plantations, "Mepkin," troubled Henry Laurens.

His main concern was that a slave named Doctor Cuffee would continue to stir up other servants, as the bondsman's mother was known to do.

Laurens was due to update fellow South Carolinian John Lewis Gervais about affairs of Congress. He noted in a letter that Gervais should sell Doctor Cuffee.

Five years training as a cobbler meant that the slave could make a good shoe, Laurens wrote, plus he could do all types of plantation labor.

Laurens advised Gervais not to sell the slave to another owner near any of his plantations. He continued to brood about the conduct of his slaves.

"... (L)et Zuma follow him immediately to sale," he wrote, "if he once more elopes or comits any capital fault."

• • •

Amid his duties as Gen. Washington's aide-de-camp in snowy Valley Forge, John Laurens found time to write his father in York Town about a plan to recruit a regiment of blacks to fight for the patriot cause.

This plan to arm and equip slaves in South Carolina gave Henry Laurens pause, despite the Continental Army's dire need for fresh troops. He was a product of the long Colonial tradition that prohibited slaves from bearing arms.

"There is nothing reasonable, which you can ask & I refuse," Laurens replied. "…But before you mature such a plan, many considerations are to be had which I am persuaded have not yet taken place in your mind. A Work of this importance must be entered upon with Caution & circumspection, otherwise a Man will be reduced to the ridiculous state of the Fox who had lost his Tail."

They would discuss the matter, the father said, when they met again.

John Laurens persisted with a plan to persuade the South Carolina and Georgia assemblies to permit slaves to serve in the Continental Army. Slaves would be rewarded with freedom for their service.

Blacks were common in northern regiments, joining as free men in voluntary service or as slaves assigned as substitutes for their owners. By one count, 755 blacks were serving as soldiers or in service roles in the Army in August 1778.

The assemblies rejected the scheme amidst, as Laurens observed, "the howlings of a triple-headed monster in which Prejudice Avarice & Pusillanimity were united."

• • •

Sawney, Cornelius Harnett's slave, was on the lam, and the North Carolina delegate was willing to pay for his return.

Attendants — both slaves and freedmen — often accompanied delegates on their travels. Among other things, their presence enhanced safety, ensuring that delegates did not have to travel alone.

The slave was about 35 years olds, 5 feet 5 inches tall, a tailor by trade with a dark complexion and his face pitted from smallpox. He wore an old brown coat, linen breeches, yarn stockings and an old beaver hat. He also was suspected of taking 100 pounds worth of goods from the quartermaster.

Harnett promised to pay $20 if returned within 20 miles from York Town or $30 if beyond that. Harnett feared that Sawney had headed behind British lines in Philadelphia.

He even sent cavalrymen out for him but to no avail.

The delegate had good reason to believe Sawney had headed east. The British actively campaigned for slaves to seek freedom behind their lines. Their plan was to create a small army of workers and impair production on patriot plantations and farms that counted on the slave labor. Often, the British reneged on their promise and resold the freedom-seekers in other colonies, enriching many officers.

"I expect to set off the middle of April (back to North Carolina), & I fear, without a Servant to attend me," he wrote to friend William Wilkinson, "as not one is to be had here as yet on any Terms."

• • •

William Alexander of Codorus Forge in Hellam Township took advantage of the Pennsylvania Gazette's Beaver at High Street print shop to place a notice seeking the return of a runaway slave.

He offered a 10-pound reward and described slave Jack Johnson as about 35 years old, wearing a small felt hat, old stockings and shoes.

"…(H)e is a fancy fellow, and much given to drink," the advertisement said. "Whoever takes up and secures said Negroe, so as his master may have him again, shall have the above reward, and reasonable charges if brought home . . . ."

• • •

Robert White, a Carlisle tavern owner, had the opposite challenge. He wanted to disown a 16-year-old slave.

His Gazette notice touted the girl as a healthy, stout mulatto wench:

"(S)he has had the small-pox and measles, can cook, wash and do most sorts of house work."

• • •

Timothy Pickering, member of the Board of War, differed from many of his fellow visitors in his view of York Town. The future U.S. secretary of state, with his servant, Millet, enjoyed his accommodations in the home of the widow of a Dutch physician, as outlined in a letter to his wife, Rebecca:

" 'Tis more difficult getting a habitation than I expected. I was puz-

In 1888, a Crispus Attucks Monument was erected on Boston Common, despite a controversy over whether Crispus Attucks, victim of the Boston Massacre, was a patriot or a rabble-rouser. Attucks, nonetheless, has been immortalized as 'the first to defy, the first to die,' and 'the first to pour out his blood as a precious libation on the altar of a people's rights.'

zled to find a place to lodge at. Finally, I was led to the widow Mihmins. But she said she had no bed but one, her own, nor could furnish me with diet. I told her I could find both. To this she consented to take me in. I am happy she did, for she is a very neat, clever and obliging old woman, and has agreed to wash and mend my linen and stockings which is a great thing here. What her price will be I do not know, but I am sure not extravagant. The old lady often puts me in mind of my mother. She is in all respects kind and motherly. I have not felt so much at home since I left Salem (Mass.). She lived all alone and now sets from morning to night till night at her spinning wheel, which, by the way, is a very modest one.

"She has one decent lower room warmed by a stove after the German fashion … and a small kitchen furnished with every utensil in pretty order. There she gets her own victuals and Millet cooks for me.

"Besides the lower room and kitchen, there is a warm chamber where I lodge. In the corner Millet has fixed me a little cabin in which he has put a straw bed, and upon that my mattress, a bag of straw makes my bolster and my pillow is upon that. I lie between my sheet doubled — the other sheet was stollen from me at Wilmington last September — my blanket lies double upon that and my great coat and other clothes over all. In this manner I have lain every night warm and comfortable.

"Millet has bought a tolerable veal at a shilling a pound, butter at two thirds of a dollar, eggs at one third of a dollar a dozen and potatoes at a dollar a bushel. But above all he gets a quart of good milk every night and every morning which with good bread at a third of a dollar — a loaf of about six pounds weight … makes our breakfast and supper.

"But half the time as we dine late, we need no supper, so we have milk enough for good puddings. The milk costs me 12 pence a quart. At the next door, Millet gets excellent beer of a brewer at half dollar a gallon. Thus, my diet is perfectly agreeable.

"I have directed Millet to get some rice and Indian meal, and when they are obtained, I shall want for nothing."

1907

article republished

Charles W. Myers wrote this piece for The York Gazette, published Nov. 24, 1907. This article, republished with photographs, headlines and story text as it appeared in the newspaper that day, is the most complete available sketch of leading black figures in York County up to that time.

The African Race in York and York County

In the rambling through the several wards in search of items that might be of interest to the readers of The Gazette, it was discovered that the colored people of York, figured prominently in its history and as the subject of our sketch for this week some interesting facts are presented, together with portraits of some of the race who are well known in York and who will be remembered in the various capacities they filled and the important services they rendered as far back as the primitive days, the parents of whom were sponsors for some of the best families in York.

'Twas but a few days ago that the name of William Goodridge was mentioned in connection with the Jordan building, occupied by Young and Busser, and in order to acquaint the younger element with his prominence the following interesting facts are presented.

William C. Goodridge

Mr. Goodridge was born in Baltimore, in 1805, and his grandmother belonged to the Charles Carrol, of Carrolton estate. Carrol was a signer of the Declaration of Independence and at York during the sittings of congress. He was always a warm friend of Washington especially during the cabal which had its quarters in York, and wose leading spirits were Love, Rush, Gates and others.

Mrs. Goodridge was born on the Carrol estate. At the age of twenty she was sold to a Doctor Goodridge at Baltimore. At six years William was sent to York and apprenticed to a Rev. Dunn, who had a tanyard in York and it was stipulated that he remain until he was 21, and then to receive an extra suit of clothing and a bible.

At the age of sixteen he went to Marietta and learned the trade of barber. He then returned to York and began business for himself. Mr. Goodridge engaged in other enterprises such as confectionary and jewelery and sold the first daily papers in York.

He had also started what was known as the Goodridge market line to Philadelphia, operating 13 cars. Mr. Goodridge lived where Rhinehart Dempwolf now resides. Mr. Goodridge built the highest house in York in centre square where Young and Busser now have their business. Here he kept one of John Browns men who made his way here after the Harpers ferry trouble.

He had his cars fixed up with hidden aparments and in this way he sent many fugitives to Philadelphia.

Mr. Goodridge failed in business but soon recovered. He did a large business and was reputed to have been very wealthy. He had a number of sons and daughters some of whom are living in Michigan and Minnesota.

The Goodridge family left York early in 1863, Mr. Goodridge dying in Minneapolis in 1876.

One of his sons is at present a prominent photographer in Michigan. A grandson in the person of Glen Goodridge resides on South Duke street.

William Goodridge, with another party named Fessel, acted as agents for the underground railroad, York being one of the stations on the route to Columbia, a party known as Black Isaac, who lived north of York, directed the fugitives to Middletown Ferry. At Lewisberry Dr. Webster Lewis, in conjunction with his father, Dr. Robert Lewis of Dover, were active spirits in the cause.

On one occasion two young Southern planters discovered three of their escaped slaves working in the barnyard of a good natured Quaker, who resided not many miles northwest of York. As they approached the mild mannered old Friend they addressed him courteously, and one of them said: "I see you have some of our boys." The farmer replied in the affirmative and said to them: "Will thee come into the house and have some dinner before thee goes?" They consented. The Quaker had three interesting young daughters; two of them prepared the meal, and entertained the visitors so well that the third sister went to the barn and planned the escape of the slaves. The Southern gentlemen finished their dinner and went to the barn for their slaves, and their surprise and astonishment was great to find they had gone, but they never suspected who assisted in their escape.

The following are the names of persons in York who owned slaves in 1780, together with the number owned by each individual:

Rev. John Andrews, 3; William Alexander, 1; Valentine Crantz, 2; Michael Doudel, 2; Widow Doudel, 1; Joseph Donaldson, 1; James Dobbins, 1; David Grier, 1; George Irwin, 3; Joseph Chambers, 2; John McAllister, 1; Widow Moore, 1; Peter Reel, 1; Michael Swope, 2; Balzer Spangler, 3; George Stoehr, 1; Andrew Welsh, 1; Bernard Eichelberger, 1.

There were 30 slaves owned in 1780 in Manchester Township, which then included West Manchester; 40 in Fawn which included Peach Bottom; William Chesney, of Newberry, who owned the ferry below New Market, 7 (he was the only slave owner in the township at that time, which included Fairview; Dover had none; Ephriam Johnson, of Menallen township, Adams county, then a part of York County, owned two slaves (one was 110 years old in 1780); Manheim, 14; Monaghan, which embraced Carroll and Franklin, had 21 (James Dill owned 9 of them); Windsor, including Lower Windsor, 10; Paradise, 2; Codorus, 5; Heidelberg, including Hanover, 14; Shrewsbury, 22; Hellam, 8; Warrington, none, as slavery was opposed by the Quakers; Chanceford, including Lower Chanceford, 21; Hopewell, 5. In the entire county, which included Adams county, there were 471 slaves in 1783; and 499 slaves in 1790. There were 77 slaves in 1800 and in 1810 there were 22. In the year 1820 there were but 6 — 4 females and 2 males. The last slave in the county died in 1841. He was owned by the father of Karl Forney, of Hanover.

In the year 1827 a large number of manumitted slaves came to York and encamped on the old commons near the old water house; among them were the familiar character of Black Rachael Dozy, Esther, Sawy and Squire Braxton. Mayor Noell during his life told many interesting incidents among them one relating to old Dozy. One morning old Dozy was coming across the chicken bridge (north George street). A number of men were washing some hats for John Demuth, when one of them accused Dozy with stealing some chickens, Dozy in his quaint style spoke, saying: "What fo 'you say niggas steal, did not de white man steal de nigga' his wife and children?" Who den learned de nigga' to steal, if de white man steal de nigga he is all right, but if a niggah steals a chicken to keep hisself and family from starvin' he's put to jail ain't dat so?" The colored camp attracted a large number of people, where old John Joice preached to the colored people, pleading with them to be thankful to their master who set them free, and more particularly to God who put it into the master's heart to set them free. The remarks of Mr. Joice caused much rejoicing among them, they clapping their hands and shouting to the top of their voices, "Bress de Lord! Bress de Lord!"

A few days after their arrival they canvassed the town in search of places for the children and succeeded well many of the children securing good places and grew up with the families, in fact raised many of the white children who grew up to be among York's prominent citizens.

Aunt Julia Johnson

The Mr. Joice referred to was the father of the well known tonsorial artist, George Joice, who does a flourishing business under the Hotel Penn.

The Joice family was one of the representative colored families of York. Mr. Joice was born in the old house that stands on the corner of Duke and Newton avenue and for many years lived in the home now occupied by Mrs. Hill and George Joice, No. 114 South Queen street and who are the only two of the living children and with Harry Woods are the last of the well known and highly respected Joice family. The Meads family on South Water street are another of the prominent colored personages who are so well known and highly respected that no further comment is necessary.

The Grays Hamilton and Thomas are known to many and years ago were the only proprietors of oyster saloons and were among the best of citizens.

Robert Butler was another of the best known and is still remembered with his big white apron as a vender of oysters.

The Foot family, one of which is Philip, is known all over the city. Another family that ranks among the best known and most respected is the Green family, of which the popular and efficient policeman, Sam Green, is a member. Philip Welsh who kept a livery where Andrew Fluhrer now resides. Mother Jackson and husband, James with the son Tommy, Charles Webster, Oliver Ramsey, Isaac Gooden, John Noble, Old William Butler, Wilson the shoemaker who had for his customers the best families of York, and whose widow is still living on Philadelphia street at the advanced age of 78 and who it is said is the only surviving charter member of the old Zion church.

Aleck McKinney, who died recently, is well remembered as an old and respected citizen, who came to York with his family in 1860. Here is Bill Hill, Sy Johnson, Bill Robinson, William Jones, Diggs the ex-policeman, George Jones and among many others of the colored race who are well known citizens of York.

The Davidge family are another of the old respected of their race who figured prominently in the best of the white families of York. One of the descendants being Mrs. Lizzie Brown wife of the well known caterer of the Lafayette club, John Brown.

Brook Sides and Brother Ben artists in the handling of the razor at their tonsorial parlors must not be passed by.

While preparing this sketch the cry of "Hot Oyster Sandwich," is heard, a gentle reminder of a prominent character known in every section of the city and by a large travelling public in the person of John Reeves who was the faithful porter at the National Hotel for thirty-one years and for the past six years the "hot oyster sandwich man," Mr. Reeves is one of the prominent members of the old Mother Church, on East King Street, and takes a great interest with many.

A conspicious figure among the colored race is the well known and highly respected superintendent of the Sunday school of the A.M.E. Zion church, Aquilla Howard, who a few weeks ago celebrated her 72d birthday. Mr. Howard came to York forty-six years ago starting with the family of John Evans and three years later went to the family of Philip Small for whom he has been their true, tried and trusted servant for forty-three years.

As early as 1810 some of the manumitted slaves located in York and about 1819 the descendants of the early colored people began to hold church under their own auspices. Encouraged by the white people they

The Rev. H.S. McMullen and family

Prof. James Smallwood

purchased a lot of ground on North Duke street and by November 28, 1819, they had a place of worship of their own on North Duke street. The first trustees of the church was John Joice, William Butler, John Linderburger, Edward Young and Israel Williams.

They worshipped in this church for over 60 years and in 1880 purchased the lot of ground on which the present church is erected from Billmeyer Small Co., and with the help of kind friends they were able to lay the corner stone on October 24, 1880, and in August 1881 were rewarded for their zeal and great interest by the dedication of a new church costing over $5,000.

The building committee were James Smallwood, G.S. Robinson, Isaac Gooden, Aquilla Howard and R.S. Welker, who labored early and late too accomplish the securing of a home to accommodate the rapidly growing congregation laying the foundation for what is today a flourishing and prosperous congregation with a well equipped church, modern parsonage and an interesting Sunday school and their financial condition such as they may well feel proud of.

The congregation numbers over 300 and a thriving Sunday school of over 200. The present pastor is Rev. H.S. McMullen, who has proven himself popular and taking a great interest in the further upbuilding of the A.M.E. Zion church.

The officers of the Sunday school are: Aquilla Howard, superintendent Albert Foster, assistant superintendent; chorister, Wilson Hauer; Organist, Geraldine Hecter, Ethel Cowles; for the Sunday school, Francis Penneyton.

The church affairs is under the able management of the following trustees: John Reeves, Wilson Hauer, Albert Foster, Daniel Craig, Richard J. Coates, Lacy Johnson, Thomas Pennington, John Bowie and Harry Drayden.

Merriman Cupit, best known to nearly every man, woman and child as "Bob" Cupit, is the subject of a very interesting sketch.

Mr. Cupit was born in Columbia, in 1828, and died in 1889. At the early age of ten he began to learn the barber business with Parry Cox Hartman. He later went to Baltimore, serving awhile with Jacques, Baltimore's noted barber. Returning to York again he began business for himself his first venture being in the Smyser property where the Security building is now located and in 1858 was doing a thriving business in the room now occupied by those prince of good fellows, Knauf and Jones, securing all the prominent people of York. In 1859 he moved into the Schroeder building now occupied by Alderman Bischop where he associated with him his son Jehu, who succeeded his father in 1899, when he moved to his present place.

Merriman Cupit, was in every sense a prominent person of his race and held numerous positions of honor and trust, all of which was acceptably filled. He was the first colored man to serve on the Grand jury, acting in the capacity of secretary, wrote the report and it was accepted by the members.

For four years he taught school in Lancaster, was a member of the colored masons and the Odd Fellows and was selected as one of an important committee by Hons. Salmon P. Chase, Charles Sumner and Henry Wilson to consider the best means for the betterment of the colored race.

Mr. Cupit was married in 1846 to Miss Jane Ann Johnson, who with her son Jehu resides on West Princess street, and is in her 82d year respected and esteemed by a large circle of friends particularly among the white people, and whose mother's portrait appears in this issue.

William Wood

Another of the persons of note was William Wood, the mention of whose name recalls his worth as a citizen.

An old and much respected Yorker that took a great deal of interest in looking after his people in an industrial point of view. He by profession was a machinist, and during these days one of the best in the city and vicinity, having worked in the same building for an unlimited number of years serving as master machinist for the following firms: Phineas Davis, Isarel Gardner, Slaymaker & Durkee practical foundry workers and builders of engines and machinery of all devisable kinds including the latest farming implements of that period. He also fitted up and put together one of the first steam railroad engines for a company in Pennsylvania to compete with engines of the same class from Mass. and Maryland for superiority.

Merriman Cupit

Jane Ann Cupit

Jehu Cupit

The engine that was constructed by him won out in the contest. It was designed and patented by one Gardner & Davis. He was a prominent member of the A.M.E. Zion church from the institution of it until the day of his death. An active member of church association G.U.O. of O.F. Having resided on Newberry street for more than fifty odd years. His son Clinton Wood was engaged in the same profession as his father, taking part in building some of the machinery that in its day was regarded as being wonderful. The machine shop in which William Wood was employed at one time was run absolutely by negro employes, that was along in the sixties.

In the early part of his history he assisted in secreting the escaped slaves to prevent them from falling in the hands of their brutal masters that may might not be returned to them for future punishment such as they had undergone for so many years.

Mr. Wood worked on the first steamboat that was sailed upon the Susquehanna river at Wrightsville and Columbia. The first spark catcher that was attached to steam railroad engines patented by Davis was built by him. He left behind him a son that was his equal as a machinist of note and respectability. He was last employed at the Farquhar Agricultural works.

Miss Susan Marrs

Attention is called to another prominent Yorker in the person of Miss Susan Marrs, who was born in York in 1809 and died in Massachusetts in October 21, 1907.

Miss Marrs was one of the most respected and trusted women of her times. She was in the employment of the families of James Lewis and Charles A. Barnitz during the early period of her life and while in their service she became generally known as "Susie." She assisted many a poor run-away slave to make his escape towards Canada the place they would always call the land of freedom and helped her brother-in-law John Johnson, to secret away those castaways over night until an opportunity availed itself to show them the road to the Big River (Susquehanna.) She left York, Pennsylvania, in the early fifties after having been around and employed at Springdale, south of York now occupied by Grier Hersh.

She was in the Lewis family when Mr. Charles Barnitz then a very prominent lawyer gave place for silk culture. He donated the grounds and building to Misses Nancy and Jane Grear who immediately set about in establishing the institution to produce the cocoons. They and Miss Cupit set about planting mulberry trees to bed the silk worms. Silk worms come from tiny eggs the size of mustard seeds and are hatched by being maintained at a temperature of about seventy degrees Fahrenheit. Soon after hatching they develop a vicious appetite for mulberry leaves and grow rapidly. At the end of about sixteen days during which they "moult" or shed their skins three times, they exude all waste watter from their bodies, leaving nothing but their two silk ducks containing their precious store and are ready for the spinner.

Mrs. Jo Ann Cupit who assisted Susan Marrs has still some of the hanks of this original silk in her possession. Miss Marrs died in Roxbury, Mass., Oct. 21, 1907. She had been in the service of the family of the late Thomas C. M. Patten of Cambridge, Mass., for more than 40 years leaving in York two nieces to mourn her loss, Mrs. J.H. Cupit and Mrs. Cornelia Noble.

The portrait of James Smallwood recalls one who was held in high esteem, as a citizen, scholar and benefactor of his race. His excellence as a worker in the church and school teacher for over twenty-five years, has long been recognized, and as a memorial to his services the schoolhouse on South Water street has been named, the "James Smallwood" school house.

Jehu Cupit, whose portrait appears, is so well known that little need be said. He was prominent among his people, identified with many of their interests and like many others, took an advanced step for the betterment of his race. Mr. Cupit has always been credited with being the originator of the first daily newspaper in York. He has, like his father, many traits that won for him the respect of the community, irrespective of race or conditions. In the succeeding of his father's business, he has for his patrons a large number of those who were customers of his father. Mr. Cupit resides with his aged mother, as a comfort to her in her declining years.

Among others who are well known were the Drowerys, one a shoemaker on South Duke street and the other a gardener for Charles A. Morris, living on South Queen, near Market.

The Schales, carpet weavers, of South Water street. The Clarks, on Philadelphia street, near George, scourers, dyers and tailors. Mother Jackson, who kept a store on Newton avenue, who had many children as customers, for "mosy", as the taffy was called.

The sketch would not be complete without the portrait of that familiar and well known personage, Aunt Julia Johnson, who is still remembered as one of the old pioneers of her race, coming to York when a child from Baltimore, but living in York for over four-score years, and at the time of her death was in her ninety-fifth year. Mrs. Johnson and her husband lived for many years with the Lewis family, and had charge of the domestics, and in fact raised the family of Lewis' and was the mother of 16 children, two of whom, in the persons of Mrs. Jane Ann Cupit and Mrs. Cornelia Noble, are still living.

1912 article republished

Dr. I. H. Betz included this sketch of William C. Goodridge and his East Philadelphia Street residence as part of a series of articles published in The York Gazette in 1912 on historic houses and buildings in York County. In "Enterprising Images," John Vincent Jezierski notes that Betz based this sketch on interviews with family members then living in York and Betz's account is the most accurate of early histories on the Goodridge family. It is republished here as it appeared in the newspaper on Oct. 5, 1912.

This mural near West Market and South Penn streets in York shows a larger-than-life William C. Goodridge, foreground, standing proudly and confidently before some of his many accomplishments — his five-story building devoted to various business lines, barbershop and rail line. Right, Goodridge is shown as the infant son of a slave and then as a young lad beginning his indenture. This mural, drawn by Don and Jared Gray of Fallbrook, Calif., is part of the Murals of York series painted on buildings in York.

The Goodridge House in York

Some years ago, in gathering material for an exhaustive sketch of the Underground Railroad in Southern Pennsylvania and more particularly relating to York county, the writer made a pretty full record of a noted-colored man whose name was well known over the country. This was William C. Goodridge whose life-long career for the most part was passed in York. He was born in Baltimore in 1805. His grandmother had been a bondwoman on the plantation of Charles Carroll, of Carrollton, who died in 1832, being the last of the fifty-six signers of the Declaration of Independence. His mother was sold as a bondwoman to a prominent physician of Baltimore. When six years of age William was indentured to Rev. Michael Dunn, in York, Pennsylvania, to learn the business of tanning, to remain until he was twenty-one years of age, and when he gained his majority was to receive an extra suit of clothes and a Bible.

It seems that the Rev. Dunn was a firm believer in work and prayer and allowed no time for anything else. It may be incidentally mentioned here as a singular incident of the peculiar changes wrought by the vicissitudes of time, that in after years, when the former apprentice had become a rich merchant, his former guardian had a hard time in traveling around the country on horseback ministering to the sinful in the towns adjacent to York, and was frequently, for months at a time, a guest of his former ward, who was a man of appreciation and accorded hearty hospitality to the good old minister.

At the age of sixteen, after Rev. Dunn's financial failure, Goodridge went to Marietta and learned the trade of a barber. He worked several years at York as a journeyman barber, when he began business for himself. He had been a bright, active and diligent apprentice. He opened his barber shop in the northwest angle of the square, in a small building one-and-a-half stories high, which, in the days of the Revolution, had been owned, by a man named Martin Brenise, who had been a janitor and bell-ringer of the old court house, which was used for the meet-

William C. Goodridge was a smart marketer. Here, he offers a remedy for hair loss.

ings of the Continental Congress, during its stay here for nine months, in 1777-8. About 1830 Goodridge also added the candy business and about 1835 added to it the sale of wooden toys, most of which he procured from Philadelphia.

He had large wooden horses mounted on wheels. Some of these horses were four inches and others ten inches in height. He also had cats, cows, lions, tigers, wolves and foxes. Some of these animals were made of papier-mache, but most of them were made of wood. These toys were imported from Germany and France, for the Americans, up to 1840, had not learned the art of making toys for children like the Germans and the French. Many of the toys would make a noise in imitation of the animals they represented. This feature was exceedingly interesting in that day, being a complete novelty. He also was the first man to keep the daily papers on sale. He sold fiddles for boys. People did not call them violins in that day.

During our Christmas season nearly every boy in town bought a mouth-organ at the Goodridge toy shop. The streets on Christmas eve were enlivened with the music from that instrument. Jew's-harps too were sold abundantly at this toy shop. False faces, later called masks, filled the front window for two weeks or more before Christmas came. These were used by the "belsnickles," who traveled through the streets, ringing doorbells and entering into the houses with masks over their faces to conceal their identity. This was real fun for the "belsnickles," but was a terror to the young of the homes, who fled to their parents for protection.

William Goodridge prospered in the toy and candy business. In 1847 he erected, on the site of the old building, a new five-story building, the highest in the town. This building, in that day of low prices, cost $6,000. The building attracted great attention, from the fact that it was built by a colored man. Goodridge enlarged his toy and candy store and also opened a barber shop. He also built and conducted a machine shop. The upper story of the Goodridge building, which was over ten feet in height, was used for more than twenty years by the Worth Infantry band and the soldiers of the organization. Hundreds of people collected on the street on summer evenings to listen to the music discoursed by this trained band of musicians, under the skillful leadership of Captain Filby. Much more might be said of the toy shop by the few older citizens who still remain. The candy shop was a great attraction to the boys and girls in the days of long ago.

Mr. Goodridge made many of his own candies. Some of the molds he used may still be seen in the hands of some individuals in the town. There are persons still living who visited his store eighty years ago. "Railroad" candy, made out of brown sugar, was a great favorite. "Newgo," made out of taffy and walnut kernels, could be seen in large quantities on the Goodridge counters. "Clear toys," in the shape of cats, dogs, lions and other animals, were in great demand. Large "mint sticks," leon, cinnamon and other candies were sold and cost one large red copper cent apiece, which was then in circulation. William C. Goodridge obtained, from the markets in Philadelphia and Baltimore, nearly every variety of candy that was sold in the country 80 years ago. No wonder that his store was visited during the holiday season before the opening of the Civil War.

Glenalvin Goodridge, his oldest son, who was still living in Michigan a few years ago, had a photograph gallery as it is now known, in this building. He first made daguerreotypes, an invention that was made by Daguerre, in France, in 1839. Later he made ambrotype pictures on plates, an improvement on the invention of Daguerre. The process for making photographs was discovered a few years before the war. Goodridge's barber shop was a popular resort for many years. He cultivated the tastes of his customers and pleased them all. He introduced the sale of "bear grease" and sold hundreds of bottles of it at 50 cents per bottle, to the Beau Brummels of the town. They believed that if they used this oil a luxuriant growth of hair would appear on every young man's crown. The bottles had a picture of a bear stamped upon the glass. Some few may still be found. Goodridge kept a live bear at his home, on East Philadelphia street, and finally killed it for the fat it produced, we are informed!

Mr. Goodridge started what was known as the Goodridge market line from York to Philadelphia, operating thirteen cars. Individual cars were operated very largely in the early days of our railroads, reaching down to the Civil war. He did a large business in hauling goods for individuals and business men in York. Some of his manifests are before us at this writing and bear the dates of 1847 and also of their conductors. The names of prominent citizens of the time of over 60 years ago are found upon them, bearing the list of articles hauled for them. They make interesting reading in the light of today.

These cars were peculiarly constructed with hidden compartments for carrying freight belonging to the Underground Railroad. The term originated in York county on the river bank. Slaveholders, searching for runaway slaves, could trace them so far, when they disappeared as though swallowed up by the earth. In perplexity, they exclaimed, "There must be an underground road somewhere!" When the railroad came into use, the term used became the "Underground Railroad." The term struck the popular fancy and became incorporated into the popular literature of the day.

His cars were used to convey several of the fugitive blacks, who took part in the Christiana riot, in Lancaster county, in 1851. These men were forwarded to Canada. His home, now owned by Mr. Rhinehart Dempwolf, of this city, was used to conceal escaping slaves. There was a movable trap-door in the kitchen floor, covered by carpet, which allowed the fugitive to find ingress into a cavern, which was filled by straw. One of Mr. Goodridge's sons described this hiding-place some years ago. When the house was remodeled a few years ago, the hiding-place was found just as he described it.

The Goodridge house was closely watched during slavery days, as the suspicion pointed strongly to him as one of the leading spirits in the workings of the Underground Railroad. Rewards were offered to those who would kidnap him and spirit him to the south, where dire punishment was in store for him. But he was a man who was fertile in resources and avoided all pitfalls that were laid for him. He was a man of rare intelligence and was self-schooled. He was also a man of great presence and an admirable conversationalist. He impressed himself strongly upon his hearers.

As a business man he was scrupulously honest in his dealings. He gave thorough attention to his business and exercised tact with his customers, who had the utmost confidence in his integrity. He had the universal respect of the community. He was earlier in life associated with the Bethel or Church of God, founded by the Reverend John Winebrenner. Later in life he adopted the tenets of Emanuel Swedenborg, whose denomination is now known as the New Jerusalem church. He was a reader of the Liberator, the Anti-Slavery Standard, Bailey's New Era, the New York Tribune and other papers relating to the slavery question, that for over thirty years was uppermost in the public mind.

He was familiarly acquainted with William Lloyd Garrison, Wendell Phillips, Gerritt Smith and most of the abolitionists of his time. His wealth, work and intelligence gave him high standing with those who were the leading spirits in anti-slavery. He was well acquainted with John Brown and the militant band that aided him. In fact one of the colored men who escaped from Harper's Ferry after that disastrous failure came to York and arrived by night at the Philadelphia street house and produced great fear and consternation in the Goodridge family.

Goodridge ordered him away from the house, as it was watched day and night at this period. In fact the southern fire-eaters tried hard to inveigle all public men who had a leaning in this direction into their net and subject them to stern punishment. Many in fact went to Canada, as no extradi-

---

BATHS.

The subscriber has just erected in the rear of his shop, a complete Bathing Establishment, on the most approved plan. It is in a perfectly private situation, and persons wishing to bathe, can be supplied at a moment's warning, with perfectly pure water, either **COLD OR HOT,** as they may desire it.

WM. GOODRIDGE.
August 29th, 1852.

William C. Goodridge's business provides baths 'at a moment's warning'.

CHRISTMAS TREE.

FOR the amusement of the ladies and gentlemen of York, and its vicinity, Goodridge will exhibit at his residence, in east Philadelphia street, a **CHRISTMAS TREE,** the exhibition of which will commence on Christmas Eve, and continue, (Sunday excepted,) until New Year.
☞ TICKETS to be had at his store.
York, December 21, 1840.

Well-decorated Christmas trees are rare enough in York that Goodridge is able to charge admission to view the tree at his East Philadelphia Street home in 1840.

WANTS.

A boy about 14 or 15 years of age, is wanted in a store.
A girl is wanted to do House work, two or three miles from town.
A boy is wanted to learn the Potting business.
A white girl to do House work, wants a situation.
A colored woman and girl, want a situation as servants.
A boy is wanted to attend a bar.
Two young men want situations as Clerks.
A good Journeyman Carpenter wanted.
A boy 18 years of age, wants a situation to learn Carpentering.
A Lady wants plain sewing.
A girl wants sewing by the week.
For further particulars apply at Goodridge's Intelligence Office, opposite the Market House.
York June 30, 1840

Eleven positions are available at Goodridge's Intelligence Office, his 1840 employment agency.

tion laws were then in existence.

Goodridge, however, through some means, hid Osborne Perry Anderson in the third story of his building in Centre Square, under the stairway in a closet for several weeks until the excitement subsided. When it was considered safe he was sent away on a Goodridge car. Anderson details these and other matters in his noted pamphlet, "A Voice from Harper's Ferry."

This pamphlet is very rare, but a copy of it is before the writer while penning these lines. Anderson was delivered, like F. J. Merriam, into the hands of William Still, in Philadelphia. Merriam had already escaped from the band of John Brown's men, who aimed for northwestern Pennsylvania. He boarded the cars at Scotland, below Chambersburg, and passed safely to Philadelphia and was met at the Merchants hotel by William Still, the colored chairman of the vigilance committee of the Underground Railroad, in Philadelphia. Two other men aimed to escape, going northward. One of these was Captain John E. Cook, who was taken at Mt. Alto by the notorious slave-catchers Daniel Logan and Cliggett Fitzhugh.

He was taken to Chambersburg jail and, although his escape was well planned, it failed through a series of mishaps. He was executed in Virginia. Another man, Albert Hazlett, reached Carlisle and was apprehended and after a determined legal contest of ten days was also delivered into the hands of the Virginians, taken back and executed. Anderson and Hazlett, of the seven men who got away from Harper's Ferry, were the only ones who escaped from the Harper's Ferry side of the Potomac. How they escaped is thrillingly related by Anderson in his pamphlet.

Anderson was a man of considerable education and was a printer by trade. He was born in Chester county. He was at the John Brown reunion of the family and friends, on the 4th of July, 1860, but returned to Canada. Twelve of the twenty-two actors of the John Brown tragedy are now buried at the big rock of the John Brown home, in northern New York. Anderson died in Washington, in 1872, some years afterward, and was buried in a nameless grave, now unidentified, in Shriner's cemetery, in Washington.

It is believed that none of the fugitives in the hands of Goodridge were ever recaptured. The Christiania men very nearly were captured, however, but escaped. Just how many fugitives passed through his hands is unknown, as records, especially after the Second Fugitive Slave Law, were not kept and those in existence were mostly destroyed, owing to the severe fines and punishment that were inflicted upon those found in the work. His fortune was largely swept away by the disastrous financial crash in 1857-8. He partially retrieved it, but the war coming on and the invasion of Pennsylvania in 1863, led the whole family to hurriedly leave the place, going to Michigan and Minnesota. The reason for this step was their underground record, which they rightly supposed would lead to their personal harm at the hands of the invaders.

After the financial disaster they still occupied the Philadelphia street house. But for the war Goodridge would undoubtedly have retrieved his fortunes. But heir removal and the changed condition of affairs militated against their return to their old home. His family embraced eleven children. But three are now living, a son and two daughters. Three brothers went to Michigan and established a business in photography after their removal from York. But a single one of the brothers is living. They have been appointed special photographers for Collier's Weekly for their section. They are also photographers for the Michigan Central and Marquette railroads.

The daughters yet living are two, Mrs. Emily C. Gray, of Minnesota, and Mrs. Mary Nicholas, of Michigan. The whole family have ever been industrious. Mrs. Goodridge assisted her husband materially in his business at York. The daughters also attended the stores. Mrs. Nicholas was educated at St. Francis Academy, Baltimore, where she became proficient in the German and French languages. The family were compelled to flee from York during the Confederate invasion, in 1863, as already stated. The Goodridge family had become so distasteful in the work of the Underground Railroad that they believed harm might befall them if they remained during the invasion.

In this surmise they were doubtless correct, as they were well known by reputation among the rank and file of the Confederates. Mrs. Nicholas learned the art of hairdressing at the hands of her father and is pursuing the calling to this day and has been very successful therein. One of the grandsons of William C. Goodridge lives in York and is pursuing the tonsorial art.

Mr. Goodridge died in Minneapolis, Minnesota, in 1873, at the age of 68 years. We do not learn of his having pursued any business after his removal from York. His had been a busy and laborious life for almost a half century. His life had its toils and perplexities and also its disappointments and disasters.

Goodridge's Shaving and Hair Cutting Saloon!
No. 49, North Duke Street, about 10 Doors from the Railroad Station.
Razors, Scissors, Knives and all kinds of Surgical Instruments put in order. Good prices paid for human hair. Wigs, Braids, Frizzetts, Curls and all kinds of Hair Work made and repaired. Hair, Whiskers and Moustaches Dyed. Grease, Tar, Paint, &c., removed from Clothing without injury to the same.   my7:65

This advertisement, published in May 1865, suggests Goodridge's business interests continued past the end of the Civil War. But it is believed Goodridge left York later that year to join other family members in Saginaw, Mich., and Minneapolis. He died in Minneapolis in 1867.

1924 article republished

This article originally ran in The York Gazette and Daily on Sept. 17, 1924. It is republished here as it appeared in the newspaper that day, headlines included.

Historical York Slave Characters: 'Squire Braxton' and 'Black Hester'

Two Noted Slave Characters Who Figured in York's Early History

Brought here in 1827

One moonlight night in the month of May, 1827, two wagons rumbled into West York from the Southland. On these wagons were about fifty negroes, who had been set free or manumitted, as the term was then used by their owners. Most of them had been owned by Quakers, who lived near Leesburg, in Loudon county, Virginia while others came from Fairfax county, near the city of Alexandria. These Quakers had been visited by Jesse Kersey, a noted minister of the Socitey of Friends, and who was born in York about 1790. He represented the American Anti-Slavery Society, and through his persuasive eloquence induced many Quakers, as well as other slave owners to manumit hundrds of colored people, who had been bought and sold as slaves before the Civil War.

There were two stories current in reference to the arrival of these former slaves. One of these, which seems to be correct, stated that they were brought here under the direction of Isaac Mendenhall, and unloaded on the York Common, being left to the care of patriotic inhabitants.

Isaac Mendenhall was a Quaker and lived in the Valley of Virginia. It would seem that his object was to have all negroes, freed by members of the Society of Friends, sent north into Pennsylvania. About the same time a colony of colored people was started at Carlisle. Many of them were freed slaves, while at a later period others were fugitives, who had escaped from their masters and were protected by friends of the Anti-Slavery Society. A large number came to Columbia, beginning in 1827, and their descendants are now there, forming a considerable part of the population of that borough.

Wants Looked After

When the negroes arrived on the York Common, in 1827, Rev. John Joyce, pastor of the colored church in York, looked after their wants and needs, and preached to them in the open air. They sat on crude benches in

19th-century York artist Horace Bonham portrays Squire Braxton and his dog.

front of him, and this faithful leader among the colored people, had the new arrivals sing with impressive effect the revival hymns which they learned in the "Ole Virginny". His solocitude for the unfortunate peopled induced the leading citizens of York to secure homes for them. The women were employed as nurses, cooks and household attendants, while the men found places as servants. Most of them prospered and remained here.

Among these former slaves, who became best known, were Charles Grange, (later called Squire Braxton) and Black Hester, both of whom lived to an advanced age. Graxton claimed to be one hundred years old at the time of his death, July 30, 1881, but it was afterwards proven that he was ninety seven. Hester lived to the advanced age of ninety four, dying in 1880. Other members of this party of slaves who are remembered were: Zach Shaw, his brother Charlie, Black Simon, Dorsey, Black Rachael, Sally Ruddens, and a few others. They became characters around town.

Coat of Many Colors

Charlie Shaw lived on North Beaver street, and was well-known on account of his jovial nature and pictureesque atire in which he walked to the colored church on Sunday. Brilliant colors attracted Charlie's attention, and the late David Heckert said that he wore

a coat of many colors, and was proud to walk up and down the streets, wearing this garment. Dorsey was one of the comical characters of the town, and many amusing stories were related of his experience in hunting racoons in the neighboring woods. All of these negroes mentioned lived to a good old age. They were older than Squire Braxton and Black Hester when they arrived in York, and that is the reason why the two, whose portraits illustrate this article, are remembered by people now living.

Story of Charles Granger

Although the correct name of the unique character known as Squire Braxton was Charles Granger, few persons knew him by that name. He was forty three years old when he landed with his companions, who reached York in 1827 after a long trip of four days in two old-time Conestoga wagons. Charles Granger was one of the drivers and he was always pleased to relate how Marsa Granger and Marsa Menrenhall had arranged to supply them with provisions sufficient for the long trip. Whether or not Mendenhall remained in York more than one day is an unknown bit of history. That he was instrumental in bringing these colored people, released from bondage to take up their abode in York has been attributed to Jesse Kersey, of York, who acquired a wide popularity down in Virginia and all through the South in preaching in favor of setting free, black people who were kept in bondage and frequently bought and sold at public auction, just like cattle and horses.

Saw George Washington

Down in Richmond in 1890, I met a sturdy negro who was eighty years old. He was reputed to have been the father of more than a hundred children born in slavery. When the male slave was set free, usually he assumed the name of his master, and the owner of Squire Braxton, who set him free in 1827, was William Granger, who lived near Alexandria, Virginia. Braxton frequently said he often saw George Washington drive up from Mount Vernon to attend religious services on Sundays at St. John's Episcopal Church in the eastern suburbs of Alexandria. He claimed to be ten years old when he often saw Warsa Washington and described the personal appearance of the first president with considerable accuracy.

Braxton had no education. He rarely attempted to read, and was not certain the he knew the letters of the alphabet. The first ten years of his life in York was spent as a servant in the home of leading families of the town. He was abstinate and did not always obey those who had authority over him; so in 1840 the Squire built a rude structure of wood, covered on top and along the sides with sheet-iron. his hovel stood on the south side of the York Common. There was a clump of trees, which seemed to be of native growth, about fifty yards northeast of the Squire's house. This grove was the resort for people to go on Sundays and while away the time with such recreation as pleased their fancy. It was not unusual for a dozen men to send a keg of beer to this grove and drink freely of its contents while discussing politics and other affairs of town and county.

Dogs his Closest Friends

Squire Braxton's closest friends at home were a dozen dogs, not always of the choicest breed, for none of them had a pedigree such as owners of dogs frequently talk about. Vicious boys would sometimes annoy the Squire by throwing stones, which alighting on the sheet iron roof, made a rattling noise. This aroused the ire of the otherwise good-natured colored man, and caused him to denounce any boys who came near his domain. He really believe that he owned the York Common, but always welcomed the arrival of a circus or a military encampment.

When the first exhibition of the York County fair was held on the York Common, the Squire became very officous for he thought that the Agricultural society was intruding upon his rights and privileges. He was given free tickets to this exhibition and then took pleasure in showing his friends around to see all the farm products and machinery brought there by farmers and manufacturers.

Squire owned a horse and wagon which he used in collecting manure and other rubbish on the public streets. After gathering a load he dumped it on a pile and later sold it to farmers or people in town who owned gardens. In this way he earned a little money sufficient to buy oats for his horse and provisions for his family, composed of himself only. He did his own cooking with pans over an open fire. In a skillet he roasted beef, which was usually given him free by butchers of the town.

Some of Squires Friends

One of the closest friends of the Squire was Martin L. Van Baman, to whom tradition says the Squire bequeathed the entire York Common, but a search through wills and deeds failed to reveal the statement. It is true, however, that soon after the Squire's death he began to improve the Common by Removing the historic home of the aged negro. From that day to the present time Mr. Van Baman has been unceasing in his efforts as a member of the Park Commission in beautifying this historic place.

Among the other "boys of 1876", and earlier, who had the honor of being entertained in the reception room of the Squire's sheet-iron castle were men whose names are known far and wide. Here are some of them, now living and if they chance to read this story, may recall other amusing incidents of the quaint old-time slave: W.F. Bay Stewart, Geoffry P. Yost, Capt. George Graybill, Horace Feesy, Daniel K. Trimmer of Chicago, Harry Winter of Des Moines, Iowa, Reuben W. Graybill of Long Beach, California, J. Hay Brown, Chief Justice of the Supreme Court of Pennsylvania, and Dr. J. Edgar Smith, Provost of the University of Pennsylvania. The "best" room of the Squire's home was used as a parlor, sitting room, library, bed room, dining hall and kitchen. All were in one apartment.

One Sunday morning when the writer of this story and a future judge of York county visited the Squire, some wicked boys fired stones which landed on top of the sheet-iron roof. This aroused the twelve dogs outside, and the wrath of the occupant that he forgot himself and called us all "dirty white trash". Finally he became composed in mind and temper and when we each gave him a dollar he apologized for his hasty words and earnestly requested us to call again.

Golden Teacher, His Medicine

While the Squire would occasionally take a drink of whiskey, he was not known to be intemperate. When he was taken sick he visited his personal friend, the late Dr. James A. Dale. Upon entering the drugstore, Dale would say: "Squire, what can I do for you?"

"I tell you how it is, Doctor, my stomach is out of order. I needs a good tonic, and you is the only man to give it. Not much money in my pockets this morning, but I want a bottle of "Golden" Teacher"; and he usually received it without pay. The Golden Teacher was aplied to a mixture of ether and alcohol and was used as a tonic in those days by other people, as well as the Squire. One bottle would cure him for a month and then he came again.

One day Doctor Dale told him that the Borough Council intended to stop him from skinning dead horses and cows for their hides and throwing the carcasses into a place on the common, which the Squire called "a horse gutter". "It is the smell from this gutter that caused you to get sick." Soon afterwards the Squire ceased this part of his occupation, but continued passing around the town with horse and wagon, gathering up rubbish. One day when the supply of oats and corn had all been used, he fed his old nag saw dust sprinkled with salt. He believed that it would take the place of oats.

Some boys on the street told the Squire that they could count the ribs of his old horse, and he could hang the harness on the hipbone at night. One day as some lads were hooting at him out East Market street, he stopped his team and went into a law office for advice.

"It is true, Squire," said the lawyer, "your horse needs to be fed better. What are you giving him to eat?"

"Wall", said the Squire, "my oats and corn is all and I is giving my horse saw dust sprinkled with salt."

Zach Shaw, a peanut vendor in York, was liberated with Squire Braxton, Black Hester and others in 1827. Shaw was long-lived, too. The estimated date of this photo is the early 1900s.

"No wonder he is poor", replied the attorney, "here take these two dollars and go and buy some oats."

"Youse the best man I met for a month of Sundays," smiled the Squire and he drove away.

Last Years of Squire

Business was dull with the Squire late in the year 1879. He had grown old decrepit, but, nevertheless, clung to life with a spirit that won for him the admiration of all his friends.

One day in September 1879 Chief Burgess John Deitch called upon the aged negro at his plain home which he had occupied nearly forty years. The Squire was sick abed and had grown despondent. While lying on a rude couch he looked up at Mr. Dietch and said:

"You have been my friend for a long time but I fear my end will soon be here. I am nigh on to a hundred years old and can recall how I was taken care of on the plantation of Marsa Granger more than ninety years ago. I wish I were down da now, for I know dat de sons and daughters of Marsa Granger, if no' livin' would take care of Charlie. Dat was de name I was called down in ol' Virginny, when I was a boy.

"Up rere you call me Squire Brazton and I have been proud of the name, but which means nothing to me now. I have lived far beyond three score and ten, which the Bible allots to man. Why, John Deitch, I remembers many things that took place near Alexandria about one-hundred years ago, now, I wonder if de good people of York like you, will take care of Squire Braxton who will soon be on de udder side of Jordan. Dat is what the colored preacher told me last night and I listened to him just like I did when I heard de white parson preach to General Washington in Old St. John's Chudch in Alexandria. I remembers when he died and somebody has told me it was in the year 1799. I yust to sit in the gallery of Ole St. John's Church with the other slaves. Marsa Granger took care of me and all de rest of the black people he owned.

"The singin' of the darkies on de plantation, I seemed to hear last night when sleep would not come to me. I though I heard one of the good old colored preachers lead off in the song, 'Swing Low Sweet Chariot, comin' to take me home."

"Ise waiting now for de engel Gabriel to blow his horn calling Squire Braxton to his long home."

These were some of the plaintive words of Squire Braxton to a longtime friend. The following day Captain Geise and John Deitch hired a carriage and took the negro to the County Almshouse. Dr. Samuel J. Rouse, then county physican, rendered medical aid to the weakened body of the old man. He recovered from this weakness and afterwards walked with two canes. After spending nearly two years at the Almshouse, Squire Braxton died on July 17, 1881.

His Last Funeral Rites

It was just as the sun was going down behind the western horizon that Rev. Thomas McGrath, astor at the County Almshouse for more than thirty years, stood in front of the grave of Squire Braxton. It was Sunday and an audience of five-hundred people from the town of York came to pay their tribute of respect to the quaint negro who had lived here so many years.

A choir of four persons from the colored church sang an appropriate hymn. Just before Rev. Mr. McGrath rose to speak, a robin perched on the topmost limb of a tree only a few yards away, sang one of his sweetest songs, just as though he had been placed on the program to take part in the funeral obesequies.

Pastor McGrath read a few verses from the Bible and then asking the audience to remove their hats offered up a fervent prayer which touched the heart of everyone who heart it. Then he spoke in a vein of impressive edoquence about the good qualities of the deceased whom he had known from the time of his early boyhood. Thus ended the career of a colored man known for half a century by all the people of York.

Potter's field, where Braxton was buried, was a tract of land adjoining the York Common, granted to the town of York by the heirs of William Penn when the town was laid out in 1741. It was mentioned in the deed of transfer that this sacred spot should be the place of burial for the worthy poor of the town and surrounding country. It was used for that purose about one-hundred and fifty years during which time several hundred bodies were interred.

When Potter's Field was granted by the authodity of the County Court for the purpose of the new High School Building, the bodies which had been buried were transferred to a selected spot adjoining Prospect Hill Cemetery.

The Story of Black Hester

The Queen among the slaves, set free in the South in 1827 and brought to York, was Hester. She claimed to have been a slave in one of the "First Families of Virginia". At that time this title was given to what was known as the arisocratic folk of the "Old Dominion", the name by which Virginia has always been known. She had been taught that eight Presidents of the United States were born in Virginia, and that made her proud of her native state.

Hester is not known to have had

Black Hester gains local renown for her good voice, quality household work and reputation for baking the best ginger snaps and Maryland biscuits around.

a surname. She would say in her quaint style to the young maidens of York, "Why bress your soul dear, one name is enough for any person. We know the apostles only by one name, and so if you call me Hester, that's enough for me." Hester had learned to read in her childhood, and for that reason she thought herself to be in a grade of society far above that of Squire Braxton, Dosey, Sarah Ann, and Sally Puddins, some of the colored folk who came to York with her in the days of long ago.

Hester had a good voice, and said she could lead the music among the "colo'ed" people before she came to York at the age of 41. Way back in 1830, one of the churches was holding what was called a protracted meeting. By this they meant a series of religious meetings, every evening of the week. The singing was one of the tones were heard over and above the women who joined in the chorus; so Hester volunteered to teach "des good white people how to sing, jis as sweet as we sung the old plantation songs down in "Ole Virginny". It was Hester's habit to call this revival a "distracted meeting", and this brought a gentle reproof from the pastor. Although, some of the neighbors said that the meetings were continued almost to the midnight hour, and when the audience was dismissed it sounded like a distracted class of people.

Late one evening, some vicious boys opened the front door of the Meeting House, and put two lambs inside. The little animals began to "bah bah", and did cause a distracted meeting. The trustees of the congregation brought suit against two of the worst boys. They were taken into court, and the Judge surprised the prosecutors by letting the boys go free without punishment. He admonished the church people that all religious services should be held before "candle light", so as to avoid future trouble, for, said the purist: "The hours between sunrise and sunset are sufficient for church services." Before 1830 nearly all religious services were held in the York churches before the sun had gone down.

Hester lived for a time near the York County Acadamy, and was employed to take care of the rooms on the second floor of the building, where David B. Prince conducted a female seminary nearly thirty years. The young girls called her "Black Hester", a name which she retained thereafter. She could give the young girls some good adivce, and she was generally popular with all of the folks who learned to know her.

Later in life Black Hester lived down on Water street. She was always in demand for certain kinds of household work, and had the reputation of baking the best ginger snaps and Maryland biscuits that could be found anywhere. "Why bress you," she would say in a laughing voice "it isn't hard to beat de bakers of this here ole town. They know how to bake bread, but Hester can beat them making sponge cake, big ginger cakes and the finest sugar cakes you ever saw."

"One day in June, 1880", said the late Miss Mary Kell, who for thirty years was a teacher in the High School, "my sister and I heard that Black Hester was very sick. We went down to her plain home and there found more than a dozen women who came to visit this quaint negro and make her comfortable.

"She died soon afterwards and a large number of people attended the funeral. The sermon was preached by Bishop Small, one of the noted preachers of the A.M.E. Church, who spent the last years of his life in York. At the time of her death Black Hester was 94.

10 ways to learn more about black history in York County

This work drew heavily from these sources as well as those on Page 95. Most of these references are available at the York County Heritage Trust's Historical Society Library, 250 E. Market St., York.

1. Hawkes, Jeffrey S., "J.W. Gitt's Last Crusade: Demise of the York Gazette and Daily, 1961-1970." Master's thesis. Millersville University, 1985. This readable academic work is the best available account of the stormy 1960s in York County. Hawkes is a journalist with The Intelligencer Journal, Lancaster.

2. Jezierski, John V. "Enterprising Images, The Goodridge Brothers, African American Photographers, 1847-1922." Detroit: Wayne State University Press, 2000.
— " 'Dangerous Opportunity': Glenalvin J. Goodridge and Early Photography in York, Pennsylvania," "Pennsylvania History," Vol. 64, No. 2, Spring 1997. These are the authoritative works on the Goodridge family, starting with family patriarch and 19th-century businessman William C. Goodridge.

3. "Lewis Miller, Sketches and Chronicles." York, Pa: The Historical Society of York Co., 1966. Miller, trained as a carpenter, left a legacy of colorful drawings with accompanying notes documenting 19th-century county life. This beautifully printed book compiles much of his work and contains a helpful index.

4. McClure, James. "Never to be Forgotten." York, Pa.: York Daily Record, 1999.
— "I saw it in the paper," 200th Anniversary Edition, York Daily Record, November 1996.
— "Nine Months in York Town." York, Pa.: York Daily Record, York County Heritage Trust, 2001.
— "No Small Matter: Politics and a Small-Town Editor." Master's thesis. Penn State Harrisburg, 1994.
— "The Murals of York." York, Pa.: York Daily Record, October 2000.
"Almost Forgotten" builds on "Never to be Forgotten," a 230-page survey of York County history. See that work's bibliography for an additional list of works consulted in writing "Almost Forgotten."

5. Smallwood, Wm. Lee. "York's 250th Celebration, 1741-1991, African-Americans of Note," No publisher, 1991. This manuscript collection brings together documents that help explain the story of African-Americans in the county.

6. "250th Chronicles." York, Pa: York County 250th Anniversary Commission, 1999. "Never to be Forgotten," Thomas L. Schaefer's "Patterns of Our Past" and

'Lewis Miller, Sketches and Chronicles' contains many valuable drawings of York's black community in the 1800s. The York County Heritage Trust also has scores of unpublished Miller drawings, including this image of the public hanging of Elizabeth Moore, a black woman, and John Charles, a French Creole.

"Builders and Heroes" make up this hardcover set. The last volume, a compilation of profiles published in the York Daily Record and The York Dispatch, is available only in this set.

7. York County Heritage Trust Historical Society Archives, File 630. This file is the best available compilation of primary and secondary sources on county black history topics. The file includes clippings from the York Daily Record, The York Dispatch, York Sunday News and other local newspapers. Recent Heritage Trust research on the Underground Railroad has augmented this already valuable resource.

8. "York County history," www.ydr.com. This section of the York Daily Record's Web site contains items from every era of county history, including 25 "Profiles in Heritage," published in the York Daily Record in 2002 and excerpted as part of this work.

9. York Gazette, Nov. 24, 1907; Oct. 5, 1912; and Sept. 17, 1924. These three lengthy newspaper articles provide the most comprehensive available insight into 19th-century black history. They are reprinted as part of this work.

10. Zarfoss, Franklin W., "Bits and Bytes of Trivia and Facts, Churches of York County, Pennsylvania." No publisher, 1996. Written as a year-by-year chronology, Zarfoss' work serves as an index to direct the researcher to sources and events for further study. The index details the day-to-day happenings in the religious community, an integral part of county life.

Other works consulted

Albright, S.C. "The Story of the Moravian Congregation at York Pennsylvania." York, Pa.: Maple Press, 1927.

Binder, Muriel and Binder, Mildred. "Life in York County." York Gazette index, 1815-1820. Historical Society of York County (manuscript), 1983-84.

— York Gazette index, 1821-25, 1984-86.

Blockson, Charles L. "The Underground Railroad in Pennsylvania." Jacksonville, N.C.: Flame International, 1981.

Bloomfield, Charles Arthur. "The Great Depression in York County, Pennsylvania." Master's thesis. Millersville State College, 1973.

Carter, Leroy, Jr. "The Bartons: Black Civil War Soldiers." Prepared for Family Reunion, 1996.

"Crispus Attucks." Public Broadcasting Service.<pbs.org>

"Crispus Attucks." The History Channel.<historychannel.com.>

Farquhar, Arthur B. in collaboration with Samuel Crowther. "An Autobiography of A.B. Farquhar." Garden City: Doubleday, Page and Company, 1922.

Gotwalt, Helen Miller. "Crucible of a New Nation." York, Pa.: York County Bicentennial Commission Inc., 1977.

Grove, June R. and Konkel, Richard K. "A History of Chanceford Township, York County, Pennsylvania, 1747-1997." Brogue, Pa.: Brogue Community Lions Club, 1997.

Hall, Clifford J. and John P. Lehr. "York County and the World War, 1914-1919." York, Pa.: Clifford J. Hall and John P. Lehr, 1920.

Hatch, Carl E. and Shirley A. Starner. "Reminiscenses of the York Hospital School of Nursing, 1894-1979." York: Strine Printing Co., 1985.

Hopkins, Leroy. "Black Eldorado on the Susquehanna: The Emergence of Black Columbia, 1726-1861," "Journal of the Lancaster County Historical Society," Vol. 89.

Kalish, Jim. "The Story of Civil Rights in York, Pennsylvania, A 250 Year Interpretive History." York, Pa.: York Audit of Human Rights, 2000.

Kammer, Ruth L. "Inside West Side: A Prelude to Memorial Hospital." York, Pa.: Ruth L. Kammer, 1986.

Klein, Philip S. and Hoogenboom, Ari. "A History of Pennsylvania." State College: Penn State, 1980.

Lapsansky, Emma. "Black Presence in Pennsylvania, 'Making it Home.'" University Park, Pa.: Pennsylvania Historical Association, 1990.

"Legacies: Remembrances of York County Women," York, Pa.: York Branch AAUW, 1984.

Library of Congress, comp. "Journals of the Continental Congress: 1774-1789." Washington, D.C.: Government Printing Office, 1906. Also available online:<memory.loc.gov/ammem/amlaw/lwjclink.html>

Mellander, G.A. and Hatch, Carl E. "York County's Presidential Elections." York, Pa.: Strine Publishing, undated.

Mount Vernon Education Resources. "Attitude Toward Slavery," <www.mountvernon.org>.

Newman, Debra L. "Black Women in the Era of the American Revolution in Pennsylvania," "The Journal of Negro History," Vol. 59, July 1976.

Nye, Wilbur Sturtevant. "Here Come the Rebels." Baton Rouge: Louisiana State University Press, 1965.

Patrick-Stamp, Leslie. "Numbers That Are Not New: African Americans In The Country's First Prison, 1790-1835," "Pennsylvania Magazine of History and Biography," January/April 1995.

Rohrbaugh, Carroll G., Jr. "Operation Underground in York County," History 21, Gettysburg College, 1953.

Sheets, Georg R. "Children of the Circuit Riders, The Story of Asbury United Methodist Church." York, Pa.: Asbury United Methodist Church, 1985.

— "Made in York. A Survey of the Agricultural & Industrial Heritage of York County, Pennsylvania." York, Pa.: Agricultural & Industrial Museum of York County, 1991.

"62nd Anniversary of the Shiloh Baptist Church." York, Pa.: Shiloh Baptist Church, 1962.

Shumway, George. "Charrette at York, Pa." York, Pa.: George Shumway Publisher, 1973.

Smith, Paul H., ed. "Letters of Delegates to Congress, 1774-1789." Washington, D.C.: Library of Congress, 1981.

Stetler, Polly. "Overnight Success: The Yorktowne Hotel at 70." York, Pa.: The Yorktowne Hotel Inc., 1995.

Still, William. "Underground Railroad Records." Hartford, Conn.: Betts & Company, 1886.

Therkelsen, Sara A. and Chanomi Maxwell-Parish. "Frances Ellen Watkins Harper," "Voices From The Gaps, Women Writers of Color." <www.voices.cla.umn.edu>

Wax, Darold D. "Negro Imports Into Pennsylvania, 1720-1766." "Pennsylvania History," undated, no publisher.

Whiteman, Maxwell, ed. "Poems on Miscellaneous Subjects by Frances Ellen Watkins," Afro-American History Series. Philadelphia: Rhistoric Publications, 1907.

Worner, Frederic William. "The Columbia Race Riots." Vol. 26, No. 8, Lancaster, Pa., Lancaster Historical Society, 1922.

Zarfoss, Franklin W. Untitled, unpublished speech on history of York County Sunday School picnics, 1997.

*For an expanded bibliography, please see works consulted in "Never to be Forgotten," York, Pa.: York Daily Record, 1999.

Index

A

Adams, John 79, 80
Albright, George S. 37
Alexander, William 81, 82
Alicea, Edwin 59
Allen, Lillie Belle 54, 63
Allen, Richard 14
Amoros, Abe 59
Ammon, Frances 51
Anderson, Marian 44
Anderson, Osborn Perry 12, 89
Andrews, John 82
Anstine, Harry B. 45
Asbury, Francis 14
Attucks, Crispus 38, 77, 78, 80
Atwater, Lewis 57

B

Bacon, Samuel 14, 15
Bair, Robert 36
Baker, Billy 57
Baker, Jackie 59
Banks, Halmon L. 51, 55
Banks, Ronald 65
Banks, Wilmon 65
Baptist, Mary 34-35
Baptiste, Ezekiel 23
Barber, Edith A. 53
Barber, William D. 51
Barnes, Bradley 65
Barnitz, Charles 12, 85
Barton, George 41
Barton, Henry E. 44
Barton, James 26, 29
Barton, John H. 41
Barton, Mary 37
Barton, Stephen 41
Bateman, Isaac 37
Batson, George 29
Bear, Alverta S. 57
Bear, William Henry 57
Beatty, Beverly 51
Begley, James W. 37
Bell, Marie White 50, 62, 72
Benezet, Anthony 8
Bennett, Woody 41, 50
Bentz, Matilda 11
Bentz, Sophia 11
Bertholff, Baron de Beleen 11
Betz, I.H. 86
Biggs, Basil 47
Black Hester 18, 64, 90, 91, 92, 93
Black, Jeremiah 96
Black Rachael 18, 90
Black Simon 18, 90
Blackwell, John A. 51, 53
Blakey III, Albert G. 55
Blauser, Doris 45
Blockson, Charles 66
Boanes, Beverly 78

Some scholars have cited 19th-century York painter Horace Bonham's best-known work 'Nearing the Issue at the Cockpit' for its objective and realistic rendering of black onlookers. The painting has been interpreted as a commentary on the social and racial barriers that are erased through sport. But some scholars have suggested that the 'cockfight' painting is a political allegory. 'It has been suggested that Bonham's variegated grouping of men and varied social, ethnic, racial and economic backgrounds represents the eligible voting population. The contest which they are so intently following is not a contest between gamecocks, but between presidential contenders Hayes and Tilden,' York County Heritage Trust research states. Bonham's real intent is not known. Washington Dorsey, right, is the subject of other Bonham works. The man with the bow tie, center, has been identified through newspaper clippings as the coachman of local politician Judge Jeremiah Black. The well-dressed man, left, is a self-portrait of the artist. Two 'Cockpit' paintings are known to exist: one at the York County Heritage Trust's Bonham House and the other at the Corcoran Gallery in Washington, D.C.

Boatwright, Mrs. Frances 47
Bones, Nathaniel 41
Bones, Oziel 58
Bones, William E. 41
Bonham, Horace 78, 90, 96, 97, 98, 99, 100
Booker, Robert 61
Borom, Dolores 55, 57
Borom, Roy O. 55
Bortner, Michael 59
Bowers, Alice 73
Bowers, Wade 59, 72, 78
Bowie, John 84
Bowles, George W. 37, 41, 47, 49, 71, 72, 78
Bradley, Margaret 11
Braxton, Squire 18, 64, 70, 83, 90, 91-93, 97
Breeland, Margaret 61

Breeland, Yvonne 61
Breland, Donnie 51
Brenner, John 63
Bressler, Charles H. 28
Brown, Hal 52
Brown, J. Hay 91
Brown, John 12, 88, 89
Brown, John (father of Brown, Lizzie) 16, 83
Brown, Josephine Elizabeth 29
Brown, Lizzie 83
Brown, Omar 41
Brown, Stephen 24
Brown, William H. 14
Buckingham, Annie K. 33
Butler, Daisy 40
Butler, Robert 83
Butler, William 35, 83, 84
Byers, Jazmin 58

C

Canty, Michele 61
Carpenter, James 37
Carr, Brad 41
Carroll, Charles 82, 86
Carroll, Geniece 60
Carter, Carol 36, 78
Carter, Leon 67
Carter, Mary Virginia 50-51
Carver, Betty L. 50
Cassatt-Coleman, Hannah 24
Cevis, Paul 53
Chambers, Joseph 82
Chambers, Karl Stephenson 37
Chapman, Mattie 55, 72, 78
Chapman, Mildred 53, 72-73
Chapman, Nesher 47
Chapman, William Russell 53,

Horace Bonham's 'Squire Braxton and the Scarecrow' shows the well-known York character on the job. Braxton, a freed slave who arrived in York in 1827, survived as a street cleaner, mixing dirt and garbage into compost, removing animal carcasses and selling the pelts. York County Heritage Trust research states: 'He lived alone in a crude hut on Penn Common and was often the target of cruel jokes and verbal abuse. The citizens of York had him committed to the County Almshouse in his later years when they became concerned that he could no longer look after himself. He died at the almshouse at the venerable age of 97, protesting to the last the notion of being placed on public welfare. An institution in the York community for over more than years, his funeral was attended by more than 500 Yorkers and was the subject of a front page eulogy in the local press.'

72-73, 77, 78
Charles, John 37, 94
Charms, Frank 38
Chase, Salmon P. 32, 84
Chase, Samuel 79
Chatman, Thomas 56
Chesney, William 82-83
Christie, Randy 59
Christine, Brad 61
Claiborne, Loretta 50, 59
Coates, Richard J. 84
Cockley, Donald J. 78
Colbert, John T. 40
Collins, Joseph 16
Cook, John E. 89
Cooper, Leo 59
Cornette, Jack B. 78
Cosell, Howard 59
Costopoulos, William 63
Cotton, Tom 9
Cowles, Ethel 35, 84
Cowles, Jesse Sumner 35
Cox, Robert
Craig, Caroline 14
Craig, Daniel 84
Crantz, Valentine 82
Crenshaw, Ray 55, 59, 63, 75

Crenshaw, Russ 61
Crew, John 15
Crispus Attucks Community Center (Association) 38, 47, 49, 51, 53, 55, 59, 60, 64, 65, 71, 72, 76, 78
Critchlow, James 37
Cummings, Aaron 29
Cupit, Jane Ann Johnson 32, 84, 85
Cupit, Jehu 32, 33, 34, 64, 84, 85
Cupit, Merriman "Bob" 32, 84, 85
Curtin, Andrew G. 17, 28

D

Dabney, Anna Mead 71
Dale, James A. 92
Dalton, John 61
Dameshek, Allan M. 55
Davis, Charles 41
Davis, Phineas 13
Deitch, John 92
Dempwolf, Reinhardt 34, 82, 88

Demuth, John 83
Dennis, Reginald 40
Devers, Jacob L. 43
Dickson, Hattie 63
Dickson, Lawrence 36
Dickson, Maria 36
Dill, James 83
Dill, Robert 65
Dinkle, Peter 11
Dobbins, James 82
Dock, Fanny 14, 16
Doleman, Chris 41, 50
Doleman, Tyrone 41
Doll, Lizzie 45
Donaldson, Joseph 82
Dorsey, Washington 96, 99
Dorson, Hetty 11
Dosey (Dozy) 18, 83, 90, 91, 93
Doudel, Michael 82
Douglas, Joseph 59, 73
Douglass, Frederick 57
Dowling, Kevin Brian 37
Downs, Jean M. 58, 69, 70
Drayden, Harry 84
Dukes, Barbara 78
Dukes, Philip 65
Dunbar, Mrs. Paul Lawrence 37

Dunbar, Paul Lawrence 37
Dunn, Michael 11, 82, 86

E

Early, Jubal A. 25
Ebert, John 78
Eichelberger, Bernard 82
Eichelberger, Eli 55
Einsig, Terry 59
Elby, Daniel A. 53
Eldridge, Roy 45
Ellender, George 29
Ervin (Erven), Johne 101
Evans, John 35, 83
Everett, Ron (see Karenga, Maulana)

F

Farquhar, A.B. 26, 39
Farrakhan, Louis 52
Ferguson, Arthur W. 40, 48
Fitton, Darnell 65
Fitzhugh, Cliggett 89
Fluhrer, Andrew 83
Fogel, Rick L. 59
Foot, Philip 83
Ford, Carrie Palmer 71, 73
Forney, Karl 83
Foster, Albert 84
Foulks, John 11
Frampton, William 8
Franklin, Walter 18
Freeman, William 29

G

Gamble, Anna Dill 36, 37
Gamboa-Taylor, Paul 37
Garretson, Joseph 18
Garrison, William Lloyd 20, 88
Gartner, Phil 9
Gates, Stacia 72
Gelzer, Timothy 65
Gervais, John Lewis 80
Gilbert, Amos 14
Gilbert, Leon 46
Gilmore, Sonja 63
Glatfelter, P.H. 39
Glossbrenner, Adam J. 54
Golden, Isaac 13
Goode, Alexander 43
Gooden, Isaac 83, 84
Goodling, Bill 74
Goodridge, Emily 20
Goodridge, Evalina Wallace 11, 17, 20
Goodridge, Glen J. 28-29, 82
Goodridge, Glenalvin J. 17, 20, 28, 29, 88
Goodridge, Rhoda 20, 28-29, 89
Goodridge, Wallace 28
Goodridge, William C. 7, 11, 12, 17, 20, 23, 28, 29, 34, 64, 70, 71, 82, 86-89
Goodridge, William O. 28
Gordon, John B. 25

Gorsuch, Dickinson 21-22
Gorsuch, Edward 21
Granger, Charles (see Braxton, Squire)
Granger, Marsa 91, 92
Granger, William 91
Gray, Don 85
Gray, Emily 89
Gray, Jared 86
Gray, Thomas 83
Graybill, George 91
Graybill, Reuben W. 91
Grayson, Charles 71
Grayson, Ida 37
Grear, Jane 85
Grear, Nancy 85
Green, Chaz Amos 58
Green, Maria 24
Green, Marian 58
Green, Robert 58
Green, Sam 83
Grey (Gray), Hamilton 20, 83
Grey, Hamilton W. 20
Grey, Jane 20
Grey, Ralph Toyer 20
Grey, Rhoda 20
Grier, David 82
Griggs, NaGus 57
Grimes, Ruth 11
Grimes, Voni B. 72, 73
Grimes, William 11, 30
Gross, Jesse M. 55

H

Hailey, Benjamin 64
Haines, Mahlon N. 71
Hale, Matthew 65
Haley, Alex 57
Ham, Debra Newman 8, 57, 66, 73
Hardinge, H. DeForest 53
Harley, McKinley 45
Harnett, Cornelius 79-80, 81
Harper, Frances Ellen Watkins 21
Harris, Joanna (Aunt Jo) 51, 77, 78
Hartman, Augustus
Hartman, Parry Cox 84
Hartzog, Ernest E. 50, 62, 73
Hauer, Wilson 84
Hawkins, Bernard 58
Hayes, Chester N. 71
Hayes, Roland W. 44
Hazlett, Albert 89
Heckert, David 90-91
Hecter, Geraldine 84
Hector, John H. 31, 34
Heeter, Geraldine
Hersh, Grier 85
Hicks, Robert E. (see Sipple, Curtis)
Hill, Bill 83
Hines, Jesse 13
Hines-Harris, Julia 55, 62, 72, 74
Hitler, Adolf 59
Holliday, Frederick D. 56

Holmes, Grelan 64
Holmes, Theodore 50
Hopewell, Henry W. 40, 71
House, Karen 65
Howard, Aquilla 13, 24, 30, 83, 84
Howard, Joseph J. 41
Howe, Sharon 63
Hunter, Bill 71
Hunter, Virginia 62

I

Irwin, George 82
Isaac, Black 82
Ivey, Waverly 45

J

Jackson Sr., Clarence 71
Jackson, James 83
Jackson, Jemima 30-31
Jackson, Jonathan 9
Jackson, Joseph 65
Jackson, "Old" Tom 30
Jackson, Tom 31
Jackson, William 70
Jacobs, Daniel 37
Jamison, James L. 49, 78
Jamison, Lance 59
Jamison, Rebecca 62
Jamison, Robert J. 62
Jefferson, James 41
Jefferson, Michael 59
Jenkins, Druesilla 48
Jenkins, Joe 59
Jenkins, Ruby Ritter 64
Jezierski, John Vincent 86
Jiles, Lewis H. 34
Johnson, Cyrus 34
Johnson, Ephriam 83
Johnson, Hannah 47
Johnson, Helen 58
Johnson, Jack 81
Johnson, John 13, 85
Johnson, Julia 32, 85
Johnson, Lacy 84
Johnson, Marshall 47
Johnson, Nathaniel 61
Johnson, Sy 83
Johnson, William A. 64-65
Jones, George 83
Jones, Singleton 30
Jones, William E. 36, 83
Jones, William Thomas 42
Joyce, John 18, 30, 83, 84, 90

K

Karenga, Maulana 50, 52
Kauffman, Carol 64
Kaufman, Adam 16
Kaufman, John 16
Kearse, Tim 41
Keenheel, Pearl 36
Kell, Mary 93
Kersey, Jesse 70, 90, 91
Kimbrough, O.H. 78

Horace Bonham's 'Opsimathy' features a young boy reading to a man. The painting's title means learning acquired late in life.

King, Dorothy 62, 64
King Jr, Martin Luther 36, 51, 52, 53, 64, 69, 74
Kirkland, Jeffrey 53
Kirkland Jr., Kerry 58, 65
Kittrell, Irvin III 61
Kittrell, Margaret 65
Kreiter, J. Monroe 34
Krupa, Gene 45

L

Lambert, Ettie 51
Lambert, Lois 71
Latimer, James 28
Laurens, Henry 79, 80
Laurens, John 79, 80
Laws, Elizabeth 36
Lawson, Leslie 52, 74
Leader, George 52
Leber III, L.P.
Lee, I.S. 37
Lee, Robert E. 25, 45
Lee, Richard 41
Lee, Richard Henry 79
Lentz, Albert P. 59
Lewis, Eli 35, 82
Lewis, Elijah 45
Lewis, James 12, 85
Lewis, Paraway 14
Lewis, Webster 82
Lincoln, Abraham 13, 24, 26, 27, 29-30, 45
Linderburger, John 84
Lloyd, Bessie E. 45
Logan, Daniel 89

M

Magida, Arthur 52
Malloy, Charles 37
Mandela, Nelson 61
Mandela, Winnie 61
Manning, Carole 36
Manning, Marylin 74
Manning, Richard 36, 51, 57, 74
Marrs, Susan 12-13, 85
Mars, James 13
Mars, John 13
Marshall, Elizabeth N. 55
Marshall, Thurgood 57
Martin, Ron 61
Maynard, Robert C. 50
McAllister, John 82
McClellan, Danny 35
McMullen, H.S. 84
McGrath, Thomas 92-93
McKean, Thomas 11
McKinney, Alexander 35-36, 83
McKinney, Sarah Sands 36
McMillan, Deborah 57
McMullen, H.S. 84

In 'Washington Dorsey and His Dog,' Horace Bonham features two different views of Dorsey, a York resident in the late mid- to late-1800s. Left, Bonham uses pen and ink, and, right, Bonham's oil painting shows an older Dorsey. Washington Dorsey is listed in city directories as a laborer. Tradition suggests that Dorsey worked in the Bonham household, possibly as a servant or handyman. Bonham included Dorsey in his multi-figure 'Cockfight' painting. Like many artists in the 19th century, Bonham worked from preliminary photographs. Renderings of that period often showed blacks in comedic situations. '... Bonham's rendering is devoid of racial stereotyping and may in fact be said to have been done not only objectively, but with friendship and affection,' York County Heritage Trust research states.

Mendenhall, Isaac 90
Menrenhall, Marsa 91
Merriam, F.J. 89
Michael Jr., Hubert Lester 37
Miles, Burgundi 66
Miller, Carrolus A. 30
Miller, Eenio 71
Miller, Eleanor 15
Miller, James 15
Miller, Johann Ludwig 15
Miller, Lewis 8, 9, 10, 12, 13, 14, 15, 16, 19, 25, 26, 69, 101
Miller, Thomas 16
Montalvo, Milton 37
Montouth, Thomas E. 38, 40, 49, 51, 63
Morgan, J. Walter 40
Morgan, James
Morgan, Mary 18
Moore, Eliza 63
Moore, Elizabeth 37, 94.
Moore, Ernest 63
Moore, George 63
Moore, John 63
Moore, Lenny 62-63
Moore, Virginia 63
Morgan, J. Walter
Morgan, James 65
Morris, Charles 14, 85

Mott, Lucretia 20
Mullen, Elizabeth 14
Murray, Stanley T. 47
Myers, Bill 38
Myers, Charles W. 82
Myers, Daisy 52, 59, 74
Myers, Davie 38
Myers, Linda 38
Myers, Milton 38
Myers, William 52, 71, 75
Myers, William E. 38

N

Newson, Gladys 65
Newson, Joseph 65
Nicholas, Mary 89
Niles, Henry C. 30
Nimmons, Henry 71
Nimmons, Isaac S. 39
Nimmons, Josephine Grayson 39
Noble, Cornelia 85
Noble, John F. 34, 83

O

Odom, Cornelius Nelson 51
Ogden, Peter 47
Orr, David M. 49, 75
Orr, Eula Mae Nimmons 49, 75
Orr, Henry C. 45
Orr, Katherine 36
Orr, M.K. 74

P

Pacheo, Jose 65
Paine, Thomas 70
Palermo, Steve 59
Parker, Montez 64
Parker, William 21, 22
Partymiller, Walt 46, 48
Patel, Parag 58
Patten, Thomas C.M. 85
Penn, William 93
Penneyton, Francis 84
Pennington, Thomas 84
Perrachia, Gabriel 37
Peters, Maurice (see Muhammad, Abdul Alim) 51, 52

Phillips, Wendell 88
Pickering, Timothy 81
Powell, Andre 41
Prigg, Edward 18
Prince, David B. 93
Profet, Lydia 14

R

Ramage, Anna 51
Ramsey, Oliver 83
Ransom, Mel 71
Ransom, William 75
Rascoe, Moses 56-57
Rawlins, Gladys 50
Rayno, Abraham 28
Rayno, Rhoda (see Goodridge, Rhoda)
Redman, Bertha 47
Reel, Peter 82
Reeves, Ivan A. 51
Reeves, John 83, 84
Reisinger, Peter 11
Rhoades, Charles 61
Rhoades, Dolores 61
Rhoades, Leroy 61
Rhoades, Raymond 61
Rhodes, Mark 59
Ridgely, Albert 16
Ritter, Abe 71
Robertson, Charles 54, 63
Robinson, Bill 83
Robinson, Ella J. 40, 77
Robinson, Greenberry 13, 36, 84
Robinson, Jackie 55
Rohrbaugh, Helen 56
Rojas, Glaed 58
Ross, Benjamin 20
Rouse, Samuel J. 24, 92
Ruby, Jeff 57
Ruddens, Sally 18, 90
Runkle, Ralph F. 53
Ruppert, Wayne 56
Rusk, David 60

S

Schaad, Carolyn 63
Schaad, Henry C. 54, 63
Schechner, Bill 58
Schonauer, Betty 63
Scott, Carl 56
Scott, Diane 56, 73
Sease, Audrey 75
Sease, Tillman 71
Seaton, Stephanie 66
Seifullah, Ahmad 61
Sexton, James 76
Sexton, John 59
Shanabrough, Lara 60
Shaw, Charlie 18, 90-91
Shaw, Robert Gould 29
Shaw, Zach 18, 90, 92
Shriver, Eunice 59
Siechrist, Jacob 16
Simmons, Edward R. 78
Simpson, Bobby 50, 51, 55
Sipple, Curtis 37

Small, Cassandra 25
Small, David 27, 29-30
Small, John Amos 37
Small, John B. 13, 18, 34
Small, Mary Jane 34
Small, Philip A. 24, 30, 83
Smallwood, James 13, 84, 85
Smallwood, Wm. Lee 1, 55, 56, 70
Smith, Amanda Berry 18, 20, 71
Smith, Gerrit 88
Smith, J. Edgar 91
Smith, Robin 65
Smith, Stephen 18
Smith, William 16
Snyder, John L. 54-55
Spangler, Balzer 82
Spangler, George 11
Spangler, Margaret 11
Spells, George 51
Spells, Wilbur 56
Spotz, Mark Newton 37
Stahle, J.A. 30
Stephens, Paul E. 41
Stetler, Nevin 55
Stevens, Thaddeus 9
Stevenson, John T. 41
Stewart, James 40
Stewart, W.F. Bay
Still, William 89
Stillinger, Clement 16
Stoehr, George 82
Streeter, Leslie Gray 61, 65
Stewart, W.F. Bay 91
Stuart, Jeb 25
Stum, Georgia 50
Sumner, Charles 32, 84
Swallow, Silas 31
Swedenborg, Emanuel 88
Sweeney, Doris A. 53, 56
Swope, Michael 82

Horace Bonham's 'Trying The Pluck' appeared as part of an annual exhibition sponsored by the Pennsylvania Academy of Fine Arts. This drawing appeared in the Academy's 1880 catalog. Horace Bonham had a varied career as a lawyer and newspaperman, but his legacy is his paintings. Many works are exhibited in the York County Heritage Trust's Bonham House in York.

T

Taylor, Levi 41
Taylor, Thomas 8
Terrell, Robert H. 36
Terry, Stephanie 62
Terry, Travis 61
Thackston, Helen L. 37, 38, 41, 75, 77, 78
Thomas, Charlie 56
Toscanini, Arturo 44
Tremitiere, Barbara 58
Tremitiere, Bill 58
Tremitiere, Chantel 41, 58
Tremitiere, Mark 58
Tremitiere, Monique 58
Tremitiere, Nicolle 58
Trimmer, Daniel K. 91
Trotman, Carlton 51, 55
Truman, Harry 46
Tyler, Roger L. 47

V

Valvano, Jim 59
Van Baman, Martin L. 91
Vogelsong, James R. 55

W

Wade, Bryan 61
Walker, Michael 60
Walker, Sandie 58
Walker, William Mae 48
Wallace, George 51
Warfield, Tim 56
Warfield, Timothy 55
Warner, Luke 64
Washington, Barbara 48
Washington, Booker T. 57
Washington, George 8, 79, 80, 91
Washington, Jeff 62
Washington, Reuben 50, 76
Washington, Solomon 39, 67
Waters, Maxine 61
Watson, George W. 45
Watts, Nathaniel 30
Webster, Charles 83
Welker, R.S. 84
Welsh, Andrew 82
Welsh, Philip 83
Wheatley, Phyllis 79
White, Mary E. 50
White, Robert 81
Whitens, L.F. 22, 24
Wilkinson, William 79, 81
Willford Jr., Aaron 64
Williams, Beatrice 36
Williams, Charles E. 43
Williams, Geraldine 43
Williams, Henry H. 43, 84
Williams, Milton 74
Williams, Israel 84
Wilson, J. Findley 47
Wilson, John Aquilla 41
Wilson, Richard 13
Winebrenner, John 88
Winter, Henry 91
Wood, Clinton 85
Wood, William 13, 84-85
Woodard, Doug 59
Woods, Bob 66
Woods, George 37
Woodward, Linda 53
Woodyard, Robert 47
Woodyard, Rosalyn 61
Woodyard, Stephen 47
Wright, James 18
Wright, John L. 18
Wright, William 18
Wye, Jural 60

Y

Yocum, William 16
Yost, Geoffry P. 91
Young, Edward 84
Young, Henry 37
Young, J.T. 41

JAMES McCLURE

James McClure, writer of this work, is managing editor of the York Daily Record. He earned a master's degree in American studies from Penn State Harrisburg, where his research focused on York County journalism history. He has taught local history at Penn State York and journalism at Penn State Harrisburg. He is past president of the Pennsylvania Associated Press Managing Editors and the Pennsylvania Society of Newspaper Editors. He is a member of the York County Heritage Trust's board of directors. His previous historical publications include: two special newspaper publications: "I saw it in the paper, York Daily Record's 200th Anniversary" and "The Murals of York"; and two books: "Never to be Forgotten" and "Nine Months in York Town." He served as general editor of the three-volume "250th Chronicles," published in conjunction with York County's bisesquicentennial in 1999.

TED SICKLER

Ted Sickler, photo/graphics editor for the Daily Record, coordinated photographs and served as principal designer for this work. He is a doctoral candidate in American history at the University of Delaware. He earned a master's degree in American studies from Penn State Harrisburg and serves as an adjunct instructor in American studies at Lebanon Valley College.

KIM STRONG

Kim Strong, Daily Record editorial page editor and writing coach, served as the primary content editor of this work. She earned a bachelor of arts degree from Penn State University and later served as adviser to the Daily Collegian at Penn State. She is a frequent presenter at regional and national newspaper writing workshops.

TRACEY BISHER CULLEN

Tracey Bisher Cullen, Daily Record graphic artist, designed many pages for this work, including the cover. She earned a bachelor of fine arts degree from Kutztown University.

DEBORAH L. HUMMEL

Deborah L. Hummel, Daily Record copy editor, edited this work. She earned a bachelor of arts degree in English from Millersville University, a master's of education degree in reading and the language arts from the same university, and holds elementary education and reading specialist certifications. She served as a substitute teacher for several years in York County school districts.

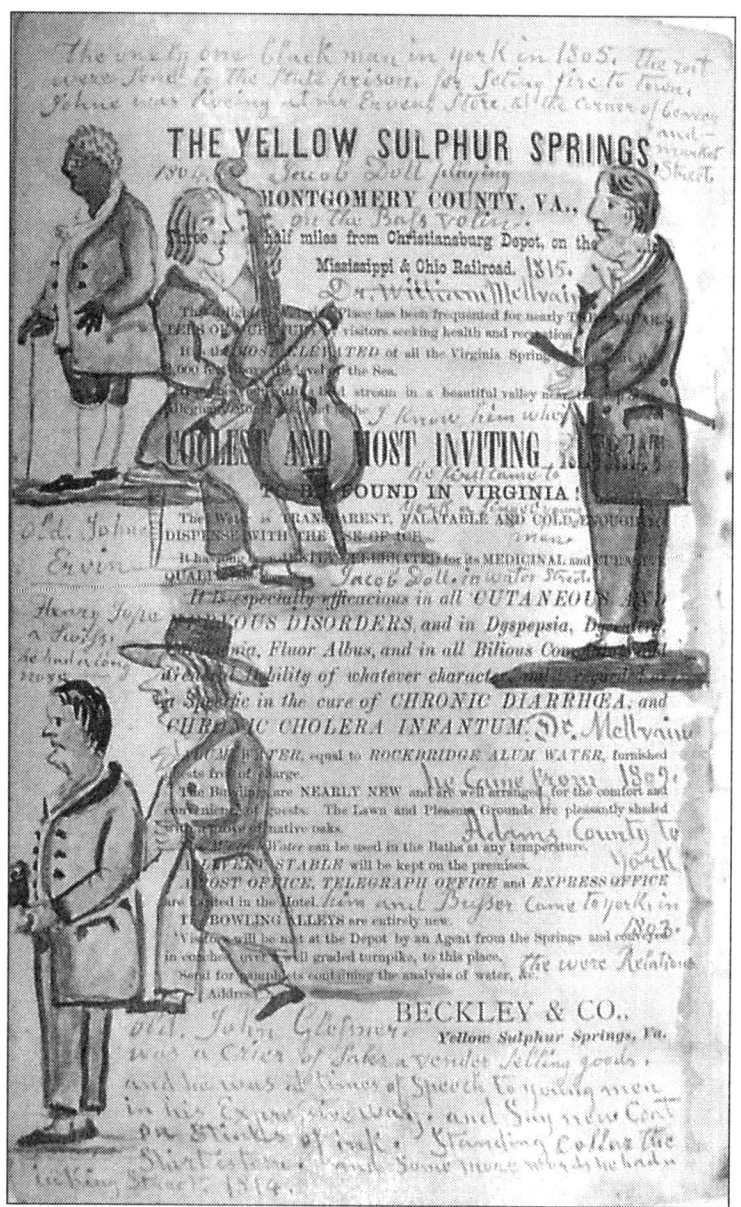

York County artist Lewis Miller has intrigued thousands in his documentation of people and places in 19th-century York County. Miller portrayed the everyday life of blacks, too. Upper left, Miller includes 'Old Johne Ervin' (spelled 'Jonne Erven' in another Miller drawing), a black from Guinea, among five figures drawn on a Yellow Sulphur Springs flier or advertisement. Miller would do his work on whatever paper was available at the time and often draw several unrelated figures on the same sheet. Ervin was not involved in the 'Conspiracy of 1803.' Miller, perhaps with exaggeration, wrote on the drawing that Ervin was the only black man left in York after the arrest of many blacks for burning barns and some houses. Much of Miller's work is in the collection of the York County Heritage Trust.